Twelve Themed
Dinners Parties from
Casa Cebadillas
Torrox Pueblo, Spain

DINNER FOR SIX at 8:00

Christopher Carnrick
and Arthur Knighton

Casa Cebadillas 627 168 943

http://www.casa-cebadillas.com

The Unique Dining Experience in Torrox Pueblo

Casa Cebadillas on Facebook

+1 239 690 6628 USA

+44 20 3286 5531 London

+1 866 660-5754 FAX USA

info@marinpropertyservices.com

(34) 627 168 943

www.casa-cebadillas.com

www.spain-vacation-holiday.com

Cover Photo

Miro Slav OtraVista Photography

http://www.mirophoto.com

ISBN: 1-4392-6501-1

ISBN-13: 9781439265017

Marylu —
You have no idea how much
it means to me to have you
here! Besos y Abrazos

Dedicated to our

Village of Torrox and all the wonderful patrons of
Casa Cebadillas who helped make this possible.

Buen Provecho

(Photo by Miro Slav OtraVista Photography, España)

In the face of doom, they used their sense of opportunity and survived.

These words have been said about Christopher Carnrick and Arthur Knighton countless times by their community in the small white washed Andalucian village of Torrox Spain. Sometimes in admiration and some, more often in exasperation or ridicule as they struggled through the economic downturn of the US dollar after moving to a small rural village in the Costa del Sol.

They thought they had achieved the "American Dream." A separation agreement after a corporate buy-out provided the way for them to move to Spain. Once they arrived, Christopher and Arthur faced the frightening facts that they sold everything, moved to Spain, unable to work and their money was declining at a rapid rate. With their tiny 300 year old Andalucian village house with a great view, a terrace, a vision and with blood, sweat and tears (more sweat in the summer more tears in the winter) they created Casa Cebadillas.

Former restaurateur Christopher Carnrick noticed there was a lack or variety with the cuisine choices in this area of Spain. Many products just were not available and many Europeans were either unfamiliar with or skeptical to try certain ethnic dishes. His partner Arthur Knighton, with over 19 years restaurant experience, was amazed how different the wait staff served diners with the absence of the motivation of gratuities. Together they combined efforts to create a unique dining experience in Torrox Pueblo.

Many tourists coming to this small village were timid to dine out because of their inability to speak Spanish or unfamiliarity of the menu items. Christopher and Arthur began preparing a traditional Spanish meal for tourists and serving them on their terrace looking out at the village, the sea and the country side. Eventually, they expanded their theme dinners bringing Polynesian Luaus, Texas BBQs and more to this tiny village and thus, Casa Cebadillas was born.

GAWD... those Americans

Growing up in America, since Arthur and I we were young, we wanted to live in Europe. We shunned many aspects of American life and during certain political administrations we wanted to flee! Once in Europe, living amongst the locals and the expatriate community with only two other known Americans we were able to see what makes us so different than others.

For all the things we disliked and for all the reasons we moved to Europe, there is something very important we have learned; we can be and should be proud of our American culture. I find it odd that this comment is coming from me, someone who ran away from home to live in a commune with an American flag sown on the bottom of his pants and not being proud to be from America. Today I can tell you, that one can be proud and should be proud to be an American. Not just for the obvious, but for our pioneering, entrepreneurial spirit which is something I never realized how uniquely American this character is, yet how important and power this quality is that shapes our country.

It is our American culture to see imperfections or voids that should be and can be, rooted out and changed or 'made right", through individual or collective efforts. Americans have been and remain quick to spot shortcomings; we struggle to find the right course and strive ceaselessly for success. This character frustrates many of our European counterparts. From the early days of its founding, the United States has fascinated the rest of the world with its distinct character — an identity and culture firmly rooted in the rising from nothing to greatness, by virtue of hard work and a little talent. As Thomas Edison said, "Genius is one percent inspiration and ninety-nine percent perspiration".

This American characteristic t often leaves many European observers puzzled, often concerned and sometimes downright angry. That sense of drive and purpose that can cause our European neighbors to wince and even chastise us that Americans don't take enough time to relax and have coffee and to be satisfied with what "is" and not to change it and just have a "stiff upper lip". The belief that dreams can come true has helped make Americans far more likely than Europeans to act and to take control of their own destinies, to take both personal and professional risks. One European scoffed at my work experience and said they were amazed that anyone with "muster" could work for more than one or two companies during their career. Most Americans have had several turns and changes during their career. As many as eight percent of Americans at one point or another have started or attempted their own business - far more than their European counterparts.

Can we be proud of everything American? Simple answer is "no". As with any society, freedom comes with a price. There are many good things in the USA, and some not so good, and some down-right shameful. However, at the end of the day, it is the pioneering spirit of our forefathers, our drive, our determination, ability to dream, to see ahead and to find the light at the end of the tunnel. These qualities are ingrained so deep in our culture that it is who and what we are and THIS, is something you can be very proud of.

Photo: Nigel Barrett, Torrox Pueblo, España Torrox Pueblo in the Axarquia of Andalucia and home of Casa Cebadillas

Preface

Upon first arriving in the village of Torrox Pueblo from the United States, we were fascinated living someplace that was like stepping back in time. Unlike our homeland of America, we found that produce was only sold when in season and ripe. Chicken had an amazing taste, eggs were fresh and olive oil was pure, cheap and plentiful. Although we relished in all the local fare there was something missing for us. Variety! We began making searches for ingredients in order to prepare dishes from other cultures here in Spain.

Casa Cebadillas was born on this quest. We began offering "themed" dinner parties on our terrace which has a fantastic view of the sea, village and countryside. After our 4th year we decided to publish the themes, recipes and tips so that others can create fun dinner parties.

The recipes contained here are from 12 of our most popular dinners. You will learn what items you can do ahead of time and prepare efficiently so you have more time with your guests, without compromising the quality of the end result. Because of our small village house, guests must walk through the kitchen to get to our terrace. What at first seemed to be a nuisance ended up being a blessing! We were forced to be prepared in advance, kitchen tidy and clean when guests arrive and again when they depart.

One of the biggest contrasts cooking in Spain as compared to the USA is the use of basic ingredients. You will not find a "cake mix" or a "muffin mix" in the store. The idea of "convenience foods" is appearing little by little, glamorized by a couple rushing into to their sleek modern apartment and popping an instant dinner into the microwave and they dine looking at a cityscape sipping a fine wine as if to say, "successful people eat this junk". If you want a cake, make a cake! It really is not difficult once you do it. My mother gave me a recipe cook from one of their clubs. We were not able to prepare one dish because everything contained some form of pre-cooked, processed or manufactured ingredient. When we return to the USA and prepare meals for friends they ask what our secret is. It is a simple secret, that anyone can incorporate into their busy schedules…go back to basics and use fresh ingredients!

Many of the utensils and products we used can be found on our on-line store to be delivered to your home on www.spain-vacation-holiday.com and select the tab for "Tienda/Store."

TABLE OF CONTENTS

Photo by Miro Slav OtraVista Photography, España

Our Philosophy of "Entertaining"

With people's busy and hectic schedules there is a growing popularity for "fast and easy" entertaining. Granted there are many short-cuts and ways that are "fast and easy" yet your guests feel "special." In our opinion there are two important factors to a successful evening, use of fresh ingredients and make your guests feel comfort and "special." We are the first to admit when someone just slaps the slop on the table and exclaims "Oh, we are all friends and family, no one really cares" we will agree, laugh and toast them however inside we felt that we just barged in on their night at home and yet WE showered, shaved and pressed clothes to attend something that turned out was not very "special."

We were once invited to a couple's house and when we entered the host was wearing a dirty T-Shirt just in from work and the hostess was standing there drinking a beer, table not set, no cooking food smells in the house, no music etc. There was no "clue" that this was an "evening" event. We wondered if we had the wrong day! A bag of chips/crisps was opened and put on the table and a container of guacamole was opened and placed on the table and we were told to "help yourselves," not a serving dish in sight. This is not entertaining. I am the first to admit that we might do this for ourselves but never for guests.

Basics: It should go without saying, but clean your house and especially the bathroom guests will be using. Have clean guest towels, put away your toothbrush, and check to be sure there is a full roll of toilet paper. Add a candle, even the battery powered candles offer some ambience. Table should be set before guests arrive. Nothing feels more awkward than arriving to a dinner party and the table is not set. Guests may look at their watch to see if they were early and the hosts were not prepared. Set your table in the same theme as your dinner party. Simple things work well. A Pirate's theme, you can scatter seashells on the table add a few tea light candles in a holder with sand and voila! Use a table cloth and cloth napkins. For a party of six there is no excuse to use paper except in the event you are having a "Trashy" theme and then by all means, just slap a roll of kitchen paper towels on the table and use an ironing board as a buffet table, open containers and place on the table and wear a dirty T-Shirt and you can declare this your theme!

Cutlery: You don't have to have a set of sterling silver to give a successful dinner party. When I first moved away from home I was thrilled at the interesting cutlery one could buy in second hand stores. You don't have to have all pieces match and you can create some very charming table settings with a mixture of patterns and styles. If you really want to invest in a good set of cutlery, looking for something that is a neutral classic design that will work for most themes. Stainless steel works just fine! If you have your hearts set on silver but don't have the cash, get married and list it on your registry… good luck! The most important part of the cutlery is cleanliness. If you find your cutlery has water spots here is a simple trick that we use. Put your cutlery in a plastic container and sprinkle with about 3 ounces of vodka. Take a lint-free clean dishtowel and buff each piece. This will remove watermarks, sanitize and make them shine.

Pot-lucks: Yes they have a purpose and depending on where you are from or your religion, they can be a custom. Funerals are one custom where people in parts of the USA bring various dishes to the family of the deceased's home. We refer to this as "funeral food." This is another time you can skip the theme and use paper napkins but under no circumstance use a black table cloth or bring out the Halloween themed setting, there is a difference between "themed" and "tacky!" If you are requested to bring a dish for a dinner party, ask the host what they would like you to bring. Regardless if it is a salad or the entrée make sure it is ready to serve. Once I had someone bring a plum pudding and they needed 3 hob/stove burners to prepare it. Another time someone brought a pasta salad and the amount was adequate for a homeless shelter and the bearer of this tub insisted that it must go in the refrigerator because it contained mayonnaise and if left out for one second we were all going to die. My refrigerator was already full! If you are asked to bring a hot dish, make it in a crock-pot and bring a serving spoon and tell your host that all you need is an outlet/power point. Dessert, bring it on a serving plate ready to serve. Do not bring something that requires the host to cut and serve and use more utensils. If the host asks you to bring a cold chicken salad, don't change it to a Tuscan Bread Salad or any other kind of salad regardless of how good and wonderful your recipe is. Some things just don't go together. You disagree? Go and brush your teeth with a nice minty toothpaste and then drink a glass of fresh grapefruit juice. Pairing food is equally as important as pairing wine with food. Your host asked you to bring something because they did not to worry about that course. Don't make the host wish they had never asked you to help.

Gift for the Host: When attending a dinner party at someone's house, it is always a nice gesture to bring a small gift or a bottle of wine. I had one friend in Seattle who would label the wine bottle with the date, occasion and guest list and store the wine away. Years later, he would host another dinner party and serve that wine, when serving he would announce what the occasion was and who was there. I thought this was a wonderful gesture. Remember that the host can be a bit preoccupied when guests begin to arrive. Don't hand over your gift and insist that they open it and gush over your gesture. Simply place the gift with a label someplace and let your host open it at their leisure. If you brought a bottle of wine, don't assume the host will serve it. It is very possible that it will not compliment the evening's meal and who knows, maybe they are saving it for the next time you come to their home!

Have a theme: A "theme" does not have to mean costumes or games during an evening. Say for example you would like to have friends over for cocktails and hors d'oeuvres. Plan your music for the evening perhaps retro lounge music, retro cocktail napkins, wear an ascot or a smoking jacket, buy a couple cocktail shakers and shake up the fun! Don't ask your guests, "What ya'll want to hear?" no one is going to agree, it feels like you never planned, and this is the quickest way to end a party. The point is when your guests arrive, they know you planned for them to be there and they will feel special. Don't mix themes! Imagine if your house was a typical "rambler" and you try to decorate "Victorian" is just doesn't work. If you are having a retro cocktail party, don't serve Tequila Shots and 7 layer bean dip with chips. There are thousands of retro recipes you can utilize from the '40s and '50s; example, home-made clam dip, little smokies and bourbon sauce in a chafing dish, fondue etc. If you want to offer something simple like beer and Margaritas, fantastic! If you don't have the time to make the guacamole, buy it and put it in a festive container, sprinkle some cumin on it and serve the chips in the brim of a sombrero. Cover the table with a bright tablecloth and buy a few prayer candles from the store for lighting and you have an "instant theme!"

Invitations: Invitations don't have to be "fancy" but should state; Who, What, When, Where and Why. Today there is a plethora of internet invitation services which offer "themed" invitations that you can email your guests. If you decide to phone your guests, make a list of who you are going to invite in advance. When you reach a guest on the phone don't begin the conversation with, "Hey, what you have going on the evening of Tuesday May 18?" you are putting the guest in an awkward position. Instead start with "Hey there, we are having some people over for dinner on Tuesday May 18th and wanted to know if you would be available to join us?" This gives your guest the option to accept or decline. We have had people ask "Well, who else is will be there?" this is why having your guest list written in advance is helpful. Although I agree it is none of their business who the other guests are, we have found that sometimes people accept or decline based on the guest list. You don't want someone declining the day before because they heard through the grapevine a particular guest was attending. Petty I know, but this is the state of decorum we live in. One reason I like on-line invitations is the host can see who has read the invitation, they can determine who can see the guest list, they can make a "theme" invitation, etc. There are many on-line invitation services available for free. Casa Cebadillas lies in an old Moorish village in Andalucía called Torrox and is difficult to find. We offer an on-line map and phone number, suggested parking and even offer to meet our guests and guide them to our house. If you have guests who have not been to your house before, make sure you offer clear directions. You don't want your guests to arrive late and agitated because they didn't know how to get to your home.

Additional guests: If you have visitors or guests when the host calls to invite you to dinner, it is best to decline and say, "We would love to come however, we have two guests visiting." This gives your host the opportunity to say, "Oh drat well maybe next time." or "Would you like to bring your guests?" Nothing puts a host on the spot more than saying "YES, great sounds wonderful, oh and we have out-of-town guests, mind if they come along?" Don't put the host in that position. If you have children, the host will have the option to invite your children or not. Same rules apply here as out-of-town guests, don't ask the host "can we bring the kids with us?" instead say "We would really enjoy attending this however it will depend on if we can get a baby-sitter, when do you need to hear back from me?" This again, gives the host the option to include them or not. We have had guests arrive with unexpected guests. In keeping with the party theme we managed to accommodate them without anyone feeling embarrassed. However, to add insult to injury the unexpected guests had specific culinary needs.

Cancelling: Emergencies can happen, however you made a commitment, so unless something drastic has occurred you need to attend. Being "tired" is no reason not to attend a party. Unexpected illness is a valid reason to cancel and your host would rather you stay home. Once at a dinner party I had a guest call and say they were feeling better and they wanted to come although they had already cancelled. I was living in a one bedroom tiny apartment. When the "unexpected guest" arrived they said they didn't feel well again and excused themselves to the bathroom where they proceeded to draw a bath to have a soak. This put a complete damper on the party let alone all of us pleading for this guest to let us use the bathroom.

Photo by Miro Slav OtraVista Photography, España

Having a "domestic" is no reason to ruin everyone's evening. Agree to be cordial at the party and then when you are in the car returning home take it back up. Once at a New Year's Eve party the two other guests had a domestic and left us with an entire dinner, decorations, champagne, caviar and lobster.

Arriving guests: If you are a guest, do not arrive early unless specifically asked by the host. If the host says 7:00 arrival time, they really mean 7:05 or 7:10. I still remember my mother declaring that a TRUE friend would never arrive "on-the dot" or GASP 5 minutes before. This is the time the host is lighting candles and double checking that everything is set for a perfect evening. We have had guests who arrived 15 minutes early because they wanted to be the first to arrive. They then wanted to chat and chin-wag. Your host has too much to do. Arrive at the stated time or 5 – 10 minutes after. If you are stuck in traffic or running late, call your host so they can inform the other guests. If you have some guests arriving late, it is difficult to have a smooth flow to the evening or serve courses. Depending on the meal some adjustments will need to be made.

Hosts: Please do not have a "couple drinks" in advance of the party. If you are completely prepared, ready and waiting for your guests, you can pour yourself the welcoming cocktail and wait for your guests to join. Answering the door already "on your way" makes the guests feel as if they arrived late.

Welcome: We found that a great way to kick-off a theme is to have a "themed" welcome drink. For example, the Moroccan Dinner starts begins with a glass of Cava with Pomegranate liqueur. Often our recipes include an "amuse-bouche" to amuse the palate. These are usually small one bite tidbits that tease and prepare the palate for the evening's dinner. This can be a "bit much" in a private setting. We have included the "amuse-bouche" and you can increase the amounts as they make a nice first course.

Atmosphere: Music is important. To be honest your guests really don't want to hear your favorite music as opposed to hearing background music, they don't have to compete with, that compliments the evening. If you are a Jazz fan and want to play Jazz music, then have a New Orleans night or play Soft Jazz and have a Sunday Brunch. Pair your music with your meal. Remember to observe your guests and if they are leaning in to hear each other, it is too loud, turn it down. The music should compliment and not dominate.

Responsible Entertaining: A host should always have a plan in the event a guest is not in condition to drive home. You should have a list of Taxi Cab phone numbers ready and available as well as cash that you can give your friend to pay the driver. If one of your guests refrains from drinking because of driving, always thank them for being responsible and always offer your guest the option to take a cab home or spend the night at your house. This way everyone can relax and enjoy themselves.

Photo by Miro Slav OtraVista Photography, España

Recipes Portions

Our collections of recipes are for 6 portions. You can increase, decrease as needed. We recommend using only fresh ingredients for a successful outcome. Recipes that offer "spicy" food, we have found that a "mild" version is best and offer sauces on the side for those who want to "bump up the heat". WARNING: My father is famous for looking for a "quick and easy" alternative and has attempted to do so with some of these recipes. The result, he usually accused me of changing the recipe! Once we eliminated each item, we would discover his "quick alternative" of which usually did not produce an acceptable result.

> *QUICK TIP Each theme dinner offers "Quick Tip" what you can do in advance to ease the tasks on the day of your dinner party.*
>
> *NOTES: My Dad is always looking to cut corners. If he has asked before if a substitute could be made, I added his query.*

Vegetarian Alternatives: Often we have a request for a vegetarian alternative for a particular diner. Not all of the meals offer a vegetarian alternative. We have included vegetarian options as well. Below is a summary of how we prepare vegetarian alternatives.

At Casa Cebadillas we are sensitive to diversity. We want you and your guests to dine comfortably with your friends and continue to maintain your lifestyle practice.

Your alternative dinner was prepared separately from the other diners. Before preparing your meal, all utensils and surfaces are sanitized and not cross-contaminated during preparation.

Different people follow different forms of vegetarianism. Casa Cebadillas defines vegetarian as one who eats no meat at all, including chicken and fish. Unless informed otherwise, we assume diners are a lacto-ovo vegetarian, or one whom eats dairy products and eggs, but excludes meat, fish, and poultry.

All ingredients are inspected to assure they contain no meat products.

Budgeting

At the time of publication, the cost for each dinner not including wine or liquor was approximately 50 Euro, 45.50 Pounds Sterling, 74.34 USD

Photo by Miro Slav OtraVista Photography, España

Twelve Themed Dinners
from
Casa Cebadillas

Pirate's Landing in Key West

To err is Human ,,,, to ARRRrrrrr is Pirate!

Welcome Aboard Cocktail

Perfect Storm or Sex on the Beach Cocktail or Long Key Electric Tea

Coming About

Tostones with Mojo sauce

Anchors Aweigh

Conch Chowder or Jolly Roger salad

Main Cabin

Jerked Pork or Chicken served with seasonal sautéed Greens and Island rice.

Final Furling

Key Lime Pie

Perfect Storm: Unleash your inner Buccaneer! This hurricane recipe is unparalleled for taste and drinkability! Everyone we've introduced it to has become hooked, and the bar that uses this recipe routinely runs out of glasses to serve in due to the popularity of this tasty beverage!

Sex on the Beach: Watch out for sand! This is a delicious fruity drink that almost anyone will like. It's a great refreshing tropical highball that is wonderful on hot summer nights or afternoons at the beach.

Long Key Electric Iced Tea: From here to Adam and Eve Bar (YES, there is a story here), this potent drink is very popular in Key West. Our version of Long Key Electric Iced Tea is a cocktail made with, among other ingredients, vodka, gin, tequila, rum, lemon and a splash of cola. It tastes like iced-tea but packs a punch like TNT!

Tostones are a twice fried green plantain similar to a thick "crisp" that you dip in a garlic mojo sauce.

Conch Chowder: In the early 1800s Conch meat (pronounced "konk" or "conk") was a staple food of the early settlers in the Keys. It was also called "Hurricane Ham." Natives of Key West, Florida and the Bahamas proudly call themselves Conchs. In 1985, the harvesting of the conch was banned, and it is now illegal to take live conch in U.S. waters, where they are an endangered species, so most conch now comes from the various Caribbean islands. We will be substituting local clams for conch.

Jolly Roger Salad: Pear halves "skulls" on a bed of lettuce with "cross bones" of brie cheese served with a berry vinaigrette "blood" dressing, ARRRRRRR.

Jerk is a style of cooking native to the Caribbean islands in which meat is dry-rubbed with a spicy mixture of allspice, Scotch Bonnet peppers, cloves, cinnamon, scallions, nutmeg, thyme and garlic. This is served with seasonal greens and rice steamed in orange juice. Sweet Potatoes can be substituted when in season.

Key Lime Pie: This famous pie is made with limes from Key West (YES we brought them back with us) in a cookie crust with whipped cream, the perfect ending to your island experience.

Pirate's Landing Recipes

COCKTAIL

All of the recipes below make one to two cocktails and are served in 10oz. hurricane glasses with ice. Mixer recipes are on page 141.

Perfect Storm Cocktail

In a Hurricane Glass with ice add:
1 oz. light rum
1 oz. dark rum
1 oz. coconut rum
1 oz. vodka
1 oz. gin
1 oz. Chambord (raspberry liqueur)
1 oz. triple sec liqueur
3 oz. orange juice
Orange slice for garnish

Sex on the Beach Cocktail

1.5 oz. peach schnapps
1.5 oz. vodka
2 oz. cranberry juice
2 oz. orange juice
2 oz. pineapple juice
Orange slice for garnish

Long Key Electric Iced Tea

1 oz. gin
1 oz. light rum
1 oz. white tequila
1 oz. triple sec
1 oz. vodka
2 oz. sweet-n-sour mix
1 oz. cola
Lemon slice for garnish

QUICK TIP: Mix cocktails in advance in glass quart jars and store in the refrigerator. This way when your guests arrive you just need to add ice and pour!

Amuse-bouche

Shrimp Cake with Aioli Cilantro Mayonnaise
This dish is our twist of a crab cake. In the particular part of Spain where we live fresh crab is impossible to obtain. As a child I was fascinated watching Rosa the chef at Bartholomew's Marina in South Padre Island Texas prepare Shrimp Burgers which these are basically the same thing only in small bite-sized portions.
½ pound raw shrimp - peeled, deveined and chopped
½ cup coarsely crushed buttery round crackers
2 TB chopped onion (shallot)
3 TB mayonnaise to bind (or cream)
½ TB prepared dijon mustard
5 dashes hot pepper sauce (e.g. Tabasco™)
celery salt to taste
1 TB parmesan cheese
½ tsp Worcestershire sauce
1 tsp chopped parsley

Chop shrimp until it becomes like ground meat. I use a small food processor for this but you can use a knife and chop fine. Add all the other ingredients EXCEPT the cracker crumbs and stir until incorporated. Now add cracker crumbs until the consistency is thick like raw meatloaf. Refrigerate. When ready to serve, heat a frying pan with 1/8 inch of oil until hot but below the smoking point. Form tablespoon size cakes, coat with breadcrumbs. Fry each side 1 minute or until golden and flip over to cook the other side. Drain on paper towels.

Aioli Sauce

I use a hand-held blender and this sauce is really fast and easy. In the blender container I add:
2 garlic cloves
1 large egg yolk
2 tsp fresh lemon juice
½ tsp dijon mustard
3 TB cilantro leaves
Blend until smooth then without removing the hand-held blender, pour into container:
¼ cup extra-virgin olive oil

Holding the blender blades to the bottom of the container, turn on and slowly pull up and by the time the blades have reached the top it has thickened! Refrigerate until serving time.

> **QUICK TIP** *NO HAND-HELD BLENDER*
> *The end result is fine but lacks the depth of the recipe above.*

Mix together until smooth:
½ cup mayonnaise
2 garlic cloves mashed into a paste
½ TB minced cilantro
½ TB fresh lemon juice

TOSTONES for 6 with Mojo sauce

3 green plantains (green but streaks of yellow)
Vegetable oil
Salt

First Frying: Cut plantains into approximately one inch pieces. In a skillet add ½ in vegetable oil and fry, turning when they are golden. Immediately remove and press each piece between the peel to flatten them out. Allow to cool. At this point you can freeze for later or you can proceed to the second step.

Second Frying: Best in a deep fat fryer but you can add one inch of oil in a skillet (cast iron is best) and then add the pressed fried plantains until crisp and golden. Immediately place on paper towels to drain and sprinkle with salt. Serve immediately with Mojo sauce.

> **QUICK TIP** *For advance preparation, after the first fry and cooling, place the tostones on wax paper, then place in plastic re-sealable bags in the freezer. When ready to serve, toss them in the fryer and voila!*

MOJO

4 garlic cloves pressed about 4 tsp
1 tsp kosher salt
6 cilantro stems, leaves chopped
1/3 cup olive oil

In a mortar and pestle, grind the salt and garlic until it forms a paste. Add the 6 cilantro stems. The stems have more flavor than the leaves. Hand grind again until a thick paste is created. Slowly add olive oil until a thick sauce is created.

Conch Chowder Soup Base (makes twelve 8 oz. servings)

1 qt. can stewed tomatoes
8 oz. tomato puree
24 oz. tomato sauce
2 tsp crushed fresh thyme (1 tsp dry)
½ tsp black pepper
¼ tsp salt
¼ tsp ground parsley flakes
½ tsp crushed red pepper
¼ tsp cayenne pepper
2 large Spanish onions (diced small)
2 medium potatoes (peeled and diced small)
4 oz. cooking sherry
1 green pepper (finely diced)
2 to 3 whole bay (laurel) leaves
2 TB olive oil

Place olive oil in large stock pot. Add onions and cook until soft and translucent. Add all other ingredients and cook slowly for 3 hours or until potatoes are soft. At this point you can cool and utilize the quick tip.

Day of the party
¼ lb. diced uncooked bacon

1 lb. ground conch (including mantle if available) or clams or mussels. We use Zamburiñas here in Spain which is similar to conch. Grind in a food processor.

Fry bacon in a large pan and when crisp, add ground conch, Zamburiñas (clams or mussels). If available, add a small bottle of clam juice. Add to heated soup base. We use a crock pot or slow cooker to keep the soup hot until serving time. The chowder holds fantastically.

> *QUICK TIP The soup base freezes really well. We make large batches and place in freezer bags each yielding 6 cups. On the day of your party, fry the bacon add the clams and add to base which has been defrosted heated and then kept hot in a crock pot. On the day of your party, you can have the soup course ready before guests arrive and can serve it whenever you are ready.*

Jolly Roger Salad

1 bottle cava or champagne
1 pkg. brie cheese, wedge wheel or stick
1 TB raspberry jam
2 TB balsamic vinegar
3 TB olive oil
Lettuce (assortment – at Casa Cebadillas we never use iceberg lettuce)
12 black olives

Peel and core pears. Slice in half to form 2 "skulls." Place in large saucepan and add the cava or champagne reserving eight ounces. Bring to a slow boil and reduce heat and simmer for 20 minutes or until pears are soft, yet hold their shape. Remove from heat. Pour remaining eight ounces of cava or champagne and place in an insulated tumbler. Sip slowly while preparing the remaining food. When asked declare it a lemon-lime soda. None will be the wiser!

To serve: On a chilled plate make a lettuce bed. Arrange 2 slices of brie about 6 inches long by ¼ inch thick to form an X. These are your cross bones. Place the pear "skull" on top and cut small indents where the eyes should go and replace with olive halves. Drizzle one tablespoon of "blood vinaigrette" dressing.

Blood Vinaigrette dressing

Wisk together balsamic, raspberry preserves and olive oil until incorporated. Taste and adjust seasonings.

> *QUICK TIP Poach pears the day before and chill with poaching liquid.*
> *Pears (1 per couple)*

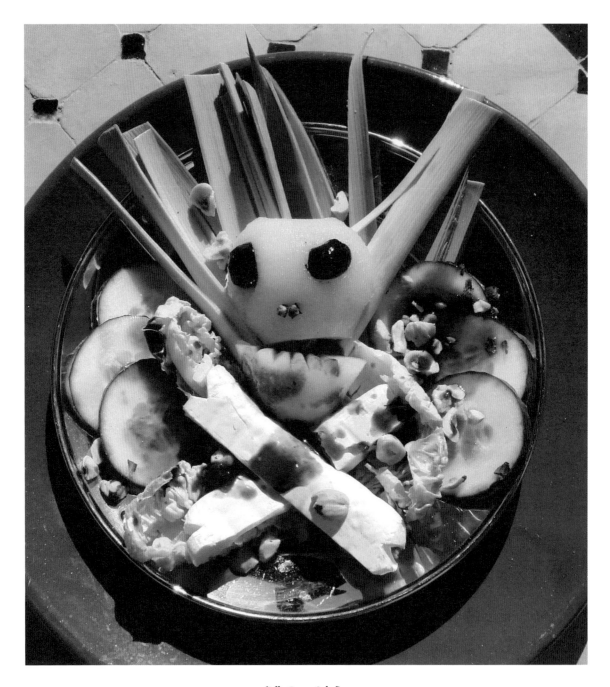

(Jolly Roger Salad)

Grissini

We always serve this course with homemade breadsticks we call grissini.

¼ cup warm water

½ pkg. active dry yeast

½ tsp sugar

¾ cup all-purpose flour, divided

¼ cup whole wheat flour

1 TB olive oil

½ tsp sea salt

1. In a large bowl, combine the water with the yeast, sugar and one-half cup of the all-purpose flour. Set aside for 10 minutes, until bubbly.
2. Stir in the remaining all-purpose flour, wheat flour, olive oil and salt and knead until smooth and elastic, about 5 minutes. Wash out the bowl and coat it with a thin layer of olive oil. Place the dough in the bowl, cover with plastic wrap and allow to rise in a warm place for 1 hour.
3. Remove the dough from the bowl and divide it into four pieces on a floured surface. Roll out each piece into a rectangle, four by twelve inches. Cut the dough lengthwise into one-third-inch-wide strips. Place the strips about one-half-inch apart on a greased baking sheet or a baking sheet lined with parchment paper. Repeat with the remaining dough. Allow the grissini to rise until puffed, about 30 minutes. Meanwhile, heat the oven to 400 degrees.
4. Bake the grissini, in batches, on the top shelf of the oven until lightly browned, about 10 minutes, rotating the pan halfway through. Cool on a rack and continue until all the grissini are baked. Cool, then store in a sealed bag, being careful not to break them.

NOTE: Grissini are easy to flavor. Add one tablespoon of finely chopped fresh sage or rosemary to the dough. Or, roll in freshly cracked black pepper, thyme, caraway, curry or other spices or herbs. Or, sprinkle the grissini with just sea salt or other specialty salt just before baking.

QUICK TIP Make these as much as two days before and keep in an airtight container

Main Course Jerk Pork or chicken

½ cup pimienta Jamaica (whole allspice berries)
½ cup packed brown sugar
6 to 8 garlic cloves chopped
4 to 6 scotch bonnet peppers chopped (*you can use scotch bonnet purée or in a pinch habanero purée and or as a last resort jalapeño purée*).
(Caution these are HOT! Use gloves and do not touch your eyes or other body parts… OUCH!)
1 TB ground thyme or 2 TB fresh thyme leaves
1 to 2 bunches scallions (green onions) chopped
1 tsp cinnamon
½ tsp nutmeg
Salt and pepper to taste
2 TB soy sauce to moisten
2 TB rum to moisten (you can add one TB to the cava you're sipping)
¼ tsp cloves
1 tsp paprika for color
Orange Juice

Place whole allspice berries in a dry blender and process until completely pulverized. Add brown sugar and process again until incorporated. Now add the garlic, peppers, thyme, scallions, cinnamon, nutmeg, soy sauce, rum, cloves and paprika. Blend. If you find your mixture is too thick and will not process, add a little orange juice until the blender motor runs and the mixture is a thick sauce.

> *QUICK TIP* You can make this marinade and it will keep for months in the refrigerator! You need to marinate / rub your chicken or pork a minimum of 24 hours in advance.

Decide if you are going to make Jerked Chicken or Pork. At Casa Cebadillas, we use ¼ quarter of a chicken, the thigh and leg. In Spain, the chickens are much larger since they run around freely until the particular morning you purchased it! Keep the size of your portions in mind when making your portions, where a quarter may work from one butcher a thigh alone may work from another. If you decide on Pork, we usually ask the butcher for loin chops or "chuletas de lomo" and have the chops cut about an inch and a half thick with the bone intact.

Preparation: Rinse chicken or pork and pat dry with paper towels. Now rub each one with vinegar. Why we do this is? Well, to be honest in Jamaica, Mary who showed me how to make this told me it was to disinfect the meat. I don't feel we need to practice this here but I still rub it with vinegar to replicate the same flavor. Now season the meat with salt and pepper. Get a tablespoon of your jerk sauce and rub all over the meat. If using chicken try to shove some under the skin. Now place the seasoned meat in a re-sealable plastic bag and place in the refrigerator for a minimum of 24 hours.

BAKING SAUCE

In a separate sauté pan over medium heat add one cup orange juice with one tablespoon jerk sauce and one teaspoon of concentrated demi-glace like "Bovril," and reduce until slightly thickened. Reserve this sauce to finish the meat. When ready to prepare light your BBQ grill and when the coals are red/white hot place meat on the rack (chicken skin side down first). When the jerk seasoning and skin are just starting to turn black, turn them over and repeat this process. Pull your grilled meat that is slightly black in areas and place into a covered metal baking pan, add the baking sauce and place in a 350 degree oven for 30 minutes. Remove from the oven and allow to rest covered for 10 minutes before serving. This will allow the juices to reabsorb into the meat.

Island Rice

3 cups aromatic rice such as jasmine
3.5 cups orange juice
1 tsp salt

First, wash your rice several times until the water is no longer cloudy. Add all the ingredients into a rice cooker and set for normal rice cooking. You can prepare this in a sauce pan but moderate your heat carefully. Increase the liquid to 4 cups and before placing the lid on the pan, add foil to assure a tight seal.

Seasonal Greens

2 lbs. Greens (We prefer chard but you can use any other variety of fresh greens. Note – spinach cooks extremely fast)
¼ cup olive oil
4 thinly sliced garlic cloves
Salt and pepper to taste

In a large sauté pan heat the olive oil over medium high heat, add the garlic and sauté until golden. Add the greens and three generous pinches of salt and pepper. Try to stir or turn the greens so they coat evenly with the oil. Cover and let simmer for about three minutes, this will allow the greens to reduce in size. Uncover and sauté an additional two minutes until the greens are nicely wilted. Remove from heat and cover to keep warm while you begin serving the main course.

Key Lime Pie

1¼ cup graham cracker crumbs or digestive biscuits crumbs
I TB roasted almonds
¼ cup dark brown sugar or date sugar
¼ lb butter
4 egg yolks
I can sweetened condensed milk (14 oz.)
4 oz. key Lime juice
After trying several variations, we found this recipe produced the best, consistent and easily served pie!

In a food processor, process the graham or digestive crackers until they are crumbs. Add almonds and process until all resembles a course meal. Add ¼ cup sugar. Pulse again until all is incorporated. Pour into a mixing bowl, add melted butter and stir. Immediately put contents into a pie tin.

NOTE - For best results and ease in serving use a silicon pie form, the second best is steel and the last resort glass or terracotta.

Pat crust and cover all areas. You can use a second pie tin to help distribute the crust evenly by placing over the crumbs and pressing down. Place crust in the refrigerator while preparing the filling.

For the filling, add 4 egg yolks and condensed milk to a clean mixing bowl. Using a wire whisk or hand held beater to thoroughly incorporate eggs and condensed milk. Now, remove crust from refrigerator and have handy a rubber spatula because this process goes quickly. Pour in the Key Lime juice and beat until the mixture becomes thickened. This will happen fairly quickly. Now pour the contents into the prepared crust and refrigerate. To serve, loosen the pie from the pan (this is why the silicon is fantastic), slice and serve with fresh whipped cream. At Casa Cebadillas we garnish with a little Pirate Flag and a wedge of lime.

NOTE - Using raw eggs. Many people are surprised that this filling is not cooked in a conventional oven. The eggs are "cooked" by the lime juice, similar to the Mexican dish ceviche where the lime juice cooks the raw fish. In Spain, eggs are irradiated and do not have the risk of salmonella. I do not suggest using farm fresh eggs for this dessert.

QUICK TIP This pie is best prepared the day before. Freezes well also!

Moroccan Mystique

Cava Casa Blanca

Cava cocktail with pomegranate juice

Hummus with Pita Bread

Garbanzo bean puree with garlic and tahini served with Arab flat bread

Slata Mechouia

Roasted Tomato and Red Pepper Salad with lemon and olive oil

Harira

Soup normally eaten during Ramadan

Tagine Djaj Bi Zaytoun Wal Hamid

*Chicken cooked in a Moroccan Tagine with home-preserved lemons
and olives served with cous cous*

Briwat Bi Tamr

*Our lighter version! Dates stuffed with cheese and mandarin orange
with a balsamic glaze drizzle*

I always love this themed dinner for its mystery and mystique. This theme is so easy to prepare, the food smells exotic and the music mysterious. You have so many options as well. You can do this entire dinner outside on your lawn, in a tent, on the floor or just in the dining room! If you want to decorate look for inexpensive curtains or bedspreads with Middle Eastern print and drape your walls or ceiling. Use lots of candles, incense and play music from Putmayo and your guests will be raving for years.

Morrocan Mystique Recipes

Cava Casa Blanca Cocktail

Cava with pomegranate liqueur :
In each champagne flute add:
1 oz. pomegranate juice
1oz. Cointreau
Fill flute with Cava and garnish with an orange peel twist.

Hummus with Pita bread

Making your own hummus - Although you might be tempted to just buy a pre-prepared container at the store we highly encourage you to make your own, its simple fresh and easy. We have tried many versions at Casa Cebadillas and have discovered that you must add all ingredients to have a good result. Do not omit items or the results are not satisfactory. The best of course, is soaking garbanzo beans overnight, drain and boil until soft.
2 to 3 cloves garlic
½ cup olive oil
2 cans or 2 jars garbanzo beans (use 3 cups dried garbanzo when soaking and boiling) drained and rinsed well
2 TB tahini
Salt and cayenne pepper
Juice of 1 lemon

Place cloves of garlic and olive oil into your food processor or blender (for a finer texture use a blender). Add the garbanzo beans. Add a pinch of salt, a pinch of cayenne pepper and the tahini. Blend until smooth. NOTE - If using a blender, and the beans are warm they blend easier if you are having difficulty getting the hummus to blend add a splash more of olive oil. NOW, the secret! Once the contents are blended you add lemon juice. Start with the juice of one lemon. I asked a Moroccan woman how to gauge the correct amount of lemon juice and her reply was that when the color lightens you have enough. When you add the lemon, blend briefly and voila… the color is lighter! Spoon contents into a serving dish, make an indentation in the middle and add a splash of olive oil, sprinkle with cilantro. Serve with Pita (plan 2 rounds per person)

> **QUICK TIP** *If you're able to purchase precooked or canned garbanzo beans you can create this hummus in a matter of minutes.*

PITA

I pkg. yeast or quick rising yeast
½ cup warm water
3 cups all purpose flour
1¼ tsp salt
I tsp granulated sugar
I cup lukewarm water

Preparation:
Dissolve yeast in 1/2 cup of warm water. Add sugar and stir until dissolved. Let sit for 10-15 minutes until water is frothy.
Combine flour and salt in large bowl.
Make a small depression in the middle of flour and pour yeast water in depression.
Slowly add I cup of warm water, and stir with wooden spoon or rubber spatula until elastic.
Place dough on floured surface and knead for 10-15 minutes. When the dough is no longer sticky and is smooth and elastic, it has been successfully kneaded.
Coat a large bowl with olive oil and place dough in bowl. Turn dough upside down so all of the dough is coated.
Allow to sit in a warm place for about 3 hours, or until it has doubled in size.
Once doubled, roll out in a rope, and pinch off ten to twelve small pieces. Form into balls and place on a floured surface. Let sit covered for 10 minutes. Preheat oven to 500 degree F and make sure rack is at the very bottom of oven. Be sure to preheat your baking sheet also.
Roll out each ball of dough with a rolling pin into circles. Each should be about 5-6 inches across and 1/4 inch thick.
Bake each circle for 4 minutes until the bread puffs up. Turn over and bake for 2 minutes.
Remove each pita with a spatula from the baking sheet and add additional pitas for baking.
Take spatula and gently push down puff. After all pita's have been baked, immediately place in a storage bag.

Alternative Baking: Using a brick oven is ideal. Build a fire inside for at least 4 hours. Remove hot coals. Toss a handful of flour on the floor of the oven. If it turns black wait 15 minutes before baking. If it turns brown, toss pita rounds in brick oven floor they will puff instantly.
Serving: If you are not using a brick oven, reheat pita on a gas flame turning with tongs until they have a couple charred marks. You also can heat a dry cast-iron skillet on high and toss cooked pita on it to heat and give a few charred marks.

> NOTE – I know many of you are groaning WHAT make your own pita, WHY? The answer is simple… flavor and appearance is really worth the effort. I promise you that this is VERY easy to make. This dinner is so simple and most can be done the day before so you may have a little time for this. If you don't or if you insist on using commercial pita, right before serving, toast commercial pita on gas range with a flame or in a dry cast iron pot until the pita begins to puff up and get a few scorch marks to look home-made, dust your face with a little flour for effect!

Slata Mechouia

This salad may appear complicated but it is not. At Casa Cebadillas, we prepared this dish for 40 people and it was very simple. We find the best results occur if you can use your Bar-B-Q grill. If not, you can always roast tomatoes and red peppers on a gas stove. In Spain, it is common to find roasted red peppers already prepared and ready too use.

4 medium roasted tomatoes
4 medium roasted red peppers
I medium red onion chopped
I lemon
¼ cup olive oil

Roasting tomatoes brings out the sweetness as well as provides a smoky flavor. Roast until charred skin cracks. Remove from heat, pull off skin and squeeze seeds out.

Roast Red Peppers until skin in black and charred. You can do this under the broiler. When the skin is blistered and charred, remove from the heat and place into a paper bag to rest. Once cool, the skin comes off easily. Remove top and seeds.

Place the red pepper and tomatoes in a food processor, add chopped red onion and pulse briefly until coarsely chopped. In a blender, add olive oil and lemon juice and blend until incorporated together. Fold this into the red pepper tomato mixture. At Casa Cebadillas we add sliced black olives for color.

> NOTE – If you are serving a large party or want your guests to chat more before the main course, you can get a large serving platter and place this salad in the middle with the hummus spread around it for a very dramatic presentation.

Harira

I love this soup. It is easy to prepare and the flavor is indescribable. This dish is normally consumed at sundown during Ramadan.

4 TB olive oil
1 lb ground lamb
1 tsp ginger
½ tsp turmeric
4 medium tomatoes cut into 1 inch chunks (may use whole canned tomatoes)
1 cup onions chopped
3 tsp salt
4 TB cilantro
3 tsp pepper
2 quarts chicken broth
½ cup orzo
4 eggs beaten
4 tsp lemon
Ground cinnamon

Brown lamb in olive oil and add onions until soft and just turning golden. Add ginger and turmeric and stir. Add tomatoes, salt, pepper and chicken broth. Return to a slow boil and add orzo. Once orzo is cooked, simmer soup for 30 minutes. Keep warm until serving time.

When ready to serve: Add cilantro, eggs and lemon juice into a bowl and mix well. Right before serving, pour into soup pot but do not stir. The result should be like Chinese "Egg Drop Soup." Place soup into warm bowls and sprinkle with cinnamon.

Tagine Djaj Bi Zaytoun Wal Hamid

6 chicken pieces
4 tsp paprika
2 tsp ground cumin
2 tsp ground ginger
2 tsp tumeric
1 tsp cinnamon
½ tsp freshly ground pepper
4 TB olive oil
The peel from 2 <u>preserved lemons</u>
1 cup green olives, pitted
½ cup water
½ cup raisins

¼ cup chopped fresh cilantro
¼ cup chopped fresh flat-leaf parsley

At Casa Cebadillas we use a chicken quarter. Here in Spain they are quite large and more than adequate for a serving. You can use any part of the chicken, however for best results keep the skin intact.

Mix spice mixture: paprika, cumin, ginger, turmeric, cinnamon and pepper. Wash and pat dry chicken. Roll into spice mixture assuring all pieces are covered. Save any remainder spice mixture. Place spiced chicken in the refrigerator for a minimum of two and up to twelve hours.

One hour before serving, prepare chicken in the following fashion:

NOTE: At Casa Cebadillas we advocate using a Tagine to cook this dish. You can get a similar effect by sealing a baking dish tightly with foil but the results are not the same. If you are unable to find a Tagine you can purchase one on our on-line store to be delivered to your front door. **http://astore.amazon.com/spaivacaboli-20**

Heat tagine either over coals or if you have a stove top model or you are using a baking dish, heat on top of the stove (hob). Add olive oil. When hot, add chicken pieces skin side down. When brown, turn over and add green olives, raisins, cilantro and preserved lemons.

*Please see note regarding preserved lemons below.

If you are using a traditional tagine, you should not need to add water since the tagine seals all moisture. If you are using another type of dish add the water.

Close lid on the tagine and cook on low heat for 1 hour.

If using a baking dish, place in 350 degree oven for 1 hour.

When ready to serve, you can present the entire tagine to the table! Sprinkle with chopped flat leaf parsley before serving.

---

*Preserved Lemons
If you have a Middle Eastern store available you can buy preserved lemons. You can make them yourself as well and they keep for months. We recommend making preserved lemons in advance to have on hand, however this is not always practical.
QUICK TIP This is an area that I admit to cheating on occasion! Get two lemons and cut into quarters. Rub one Tablespoon of kosher salt all over the pieces and place in a small microwavable container. Add juice from a jar of green olives. Microwave for two minutes covered. Let rest for fifteen minutes. Microwave again for two minutes and allow to rest. When the skin is soft they are ready to use.

Cous Cous

Making cous cous that is flakey and soft is easy as long as you don't follow the instructions on the box! Through trial and error we have finally developed a method that has produced a perfect product each time.

3 cups medium grain cous cous
3 cups water
2 chicken or beef bouillon cubes
2 TB olive oil
Salt to taste

Put cous cous in a large bowl. Put olive oil in your hands. Now pick up handfuls of cous cous and rub it letting it fall back into the bowl and coating each piece of cous cous. Repeat this process until all grains are coated.

In a large baking dish heat water and bouillon until it starts to boil. Remove from heat. Slowly pour cous cous into the hot water evenly. Loosely cover and return to low heat until steam comes through the cous cous, you can also put the baking dish in the oven at 350 degrees until steam comes through the cous cous. Once steam has traveled through the cous cous (should take 5 minutes) it is done. Add a pat of butter and fluff with a fork.

Briwat Bi Tamr

18 dates
18 pieces brie cheese
18 mandarin orange slices
½ cup balsamic vinegar

This is a much lighter version than the original and it is a perfect ending to this meal.

Place three pitted dates on each plate and stuff each date with one piece brie and one orange slice.

On the stovetop, heat balsamic vinegar until it reduces by half and becomes thick like a syrup.

Now drizzle all over the dates and serve immediately.

QUICK TIP You can prepare the balsamic in advance and keep in a container in the refrigerator. When ready to serve the dessert, place the container in the microwave for five to ten seconds or slightly less thick than honey. CAUTION, if heated too much the glaze will be too thin.

Arabic Influences

Alibaba Alibi

Lemon and mint scented vodka Cava Cocktail

Baba Ghanouj with Pita bread

Grill Roasted Aubergine puree with garlic and tahini
served with Arab flat bread

Slata Tabbouleh

Bulgar salad with mint, lemon and olive oil served in lettuce pockets

Tagine Bil Barkok Wal Loz

Lamb shank slow roasted in a Moroccan Tagine
with prunes and almonds, served with cous cous

Yogurtlu Tatlisi

Light and airy yogurt cake served with a citrus sauce

This theme can be decorated the same as the Moroccan however add Belly Dancing music and encourage guests to come in costume or "fancy dress." The best part of wearing Jalabas is you don't have a belt and you can eat without feeling uncomfortable! At Casa Cebadillas we use lots of candles and add a Hookah in the center of the table and place a piece of charcoal with incense of myrrh, mint or frankincense.

Arabic Influences Recipes

Alibaba Alibi

1 cup lemon sorbet
1 TB finely chopped fresh mint
½ cup Citron vodka

Mix one cup of softened lemon sorbet in a plastic container. Add mint and vodka and stir and immediately replace in the freezer for at least 4 hours.

When ready to serve, divide the container into 6 portions and add each portion of the lemon mint sorbet into 6 champagne flutes. Top with Cava and garnish with a sprig of fresh mint.

Baba Ghanouj with Pita bread

1 lb. eggplant (aubergine)
Olive Oil
1 garlic clove crushed
2 TB tahini
1 lemon juiced, 3TB
1 TB Olive Oil
Pinch of salt
Fresh Parsley

Pita 2 rounds pp* See previous pita bread recipe
Place oven rack approximately 6 inches from broiler. Pierce the eggplant several times with a fork and rub with olive oil and place on a baking sheet. Broil the eggplant for about 45 minutes turning the eggplant as the skin begins to char on each side. The eggplant will become deflated and soft. Remove from oven and allow to cool.

Meanwhile, place the crushed garlic, tahini and lemon juice in a mixing bowl (if using handheld blender), food processor or blender. When the eggplant has cooled, slice it open lengthwise and scoop out the pulp directly into the food processor being careful not to scoop all the way through the skin. Discard skins and blend for about 30 seconds, add salt to taste and pulse through the mixture. Once you have sliced open the eggplant, it is important to get the flesh into the lemon juice quickly to prevent it from turning dark.

You can make the item ahead of time and keep in the refrigerator. When ready to serve spoon into a bowl garnish with a drizzle of olive oil and chopped fresh parsley. Serve with pita bread.

Slata Tabbouleh

1 cup bulgar
½ cup boiled water
1 TB tomato paste
Juice of 1½ lemons
5 TB olive oil
1 fresh red pepper
1 fresh green pepper
Salt
5 to 7 scallions chopped including the green tops
3 tomatoes seeded and diced
¼ cup chopped parsley
3 TB mint leaves chopped
Lettuce leaf cups (such as Belgium endive or baby bib lettuce)

In a medium bowl add bulgar and boiled water, set-aside for 30 minutes. Mix remaining ingredients except the lettuce leaves. Add to bulgar and toss.

To serve: On each plate fill a lettuce cup with Tabbouleh salad and serve.

QUICK TIP Make this salad the night before to let the flavor meld together.

Tagine Bil Barkok Wal Loz

Please read previous menu regarding tagines
6 Lamb Shanks (Can use pork loin but this is far from authentic and forbidden in Arabic culture!)
1 onion cut in slivers
2 garlic cloves minced
1 tsp ginger
½ tsp saffron
Salt and pepper
2 tsp cinnamon
Beef broth
Honey (touch)

2 cups prunes
Garnish blanched almonds, sesame seeds, pine nuts
Cous Cous

Season the lamb or pork with ginger, saffron, cinnamon, salt and pepper. Place lamb in hot tagine and add enough broth to cover half way up the meat. Cover and cook for 25 minutes. Remove cover and add prunes, replace cover and cook an additional 15 minutes.

Drizzle a small amount of honey on each piece of lamb or pork and sprinkle with almonds, sesame seeds or pine nuts. Serve with cous cous.

Cous Cous: *See previous menu for recipe.*

Yogurtlu Tatlisi for six

4 eggs separated
½ cup sugar
3 TB flour
1 2/3 cup Greek yogurt
Zest of 1 lemon
SAUCE
2/3 cup water
1¼ cup sugar
1 TB lemon juice
Grated zest of orange
Preheat oven to 350.

Beat egg yolks with flour until smooth. Add yogurt and lemon zest and beat again until incorporated. In a separate bowl, preferably copper, whip the egg whites until they form soft foamy peaks. Add sugar and continue to beat until stiff peaks are formed. Fold egg whites and yogurt mixture carefully. Pour into a greased spring-form pan and bake until it has risen in the middle and has a few brown spots. It will rise like a soufflé.

Sauce: In a saucepan add water, sugar, lemon juice and orange zest. Boil until it becomes syrupy.

To serve: Serve cake room temperature or slightly warm. Remove spring-form and slice cake into serving portions. Drizzle citrus sauce on each piece.

Texas BBQ Hee Haw

Valley Peach Daiquiri or Texas Blue Margarita

Great Plains Maize Nuts

Chili Spiced Corn Nuts

Armadillo Eggs

Deviled Quail Eggs Texas Style with a Jalapeño Kiss

Lake Thomas BBQ Chicken

Texas BBQ Chicken cooked on the Grill

Tahoka Highway Cole Slaw and Baptist Potluck Potato Salad

Anyone who was attended a Texas Baptist Church Social will know what these are! Shredded Cabbage with a sour cream dressing and cold potatoes with house dressing and pickles

King Ranch Cornbread

Traditional Texas quick bread made with corn flour and cooked in a cast iron pan.

Needless Mark-up Pralines

Texas Famous Confection

Cerveza and Texas Tea

Growing up in the plains of west Texas, I had the opportunity to attend many BBQs, church socials and potlucks. Although from pictures and photos one could come to the conclusion that Texans don't really care about a BBQ party or the formality of a party… but quite the contrary, a Texas BBQ is more than "grilling." It is a fine art. Beverage service is not "just a beer," it is carefully selected and paired as if a fine wine. Margarita's are rarely from a mix and the best tequila is used. BBQ sauce is never purchased but rather a handed down secret from family to be enjoyed. Texans will come across that their BBQ was just "nut'n special, just family and friends" but the truth is, a great deal of work and preparation was spent to create a big ole Texas BBQ.

Décor for this theme is VERY easy. You can even take a wooden door off the hinges on a couple saw horses for a table. Use bandanas for napkins and tie each one with thick twine. Serve drinks in mason jars and use cast iron for accents. You can even get a cowboy hat and place upside down on the table and add an terracotta pot of cactus for a center piece. Country and western music in the back ground and all your prairie doggies will be yell HEE HAW!

Texas BBQ Recipes

Texas Blue Margarita

2 oz. tequila
1 oz. blue curaçao
4 oz. margarita mix (see recipe page …)

You can shake all the ingredients in a martini shaker and pour over ice or you can place all ingredients in a blender with ice and blend. Don't put in too much ice in at first, while blending drop ice into the blender a few cubes at a time until it the mixture becomes thick but smooth, making it an adult slushee. Garnish with a lime wedge.

Valley Peach Daiquiri (6 Daiquiris)

12 oz white rum
6 oz Peach Schnapps
6 Fresh Peaches, skin and pits removed
6 oz, Sweet and Sour (see recipe page …)

Place all ingredients into a blender and process until liquid. Pour over ice. Alternatively, add ice cubes in the blender and process and make a frozen daiquiri! You can omit the alcohol for any designated drivers!

> *NOTE – To easily remove the skin from a fresh peach, place in a sauce pan of boiling water for one full minute, remove and drop into an ice-water bath. The skin will slip right off!*

Great Plains Maize Nuts

1 large pkg. corn nuts (plain flavor)
1 TB chili blend
1 TB butter

Heat butter in a cast-iron or heavy bottomed pan, when melted and bubbling, but not brown, toss in corn nuts. Remove from heat. Stir in chili powder until corn nuts are coated. Place on paper towels and store in an airtight container until ready to serve.

Armadillo Eggs

6 large eggs, hard boiled
¼ cup mayonnaise
1 tsp brown or yellow mustard
¼ cup finely chopped jalapeño peppers
Salt and pepper to taste
Paprika to garnish
At Casa Cebadillas we use quail eggs which are plentiful here but you can use chicken eggs.

Hard boil eggs and cool. Cut in half, remove yolks and add to a bowl with the remaining ingredients. When ready to serve, stuff egg halves, sprinkle with paprika and serve.

> *QUICK TIP: We make the filling in a plastic re-sealable storage bag using our fingers to mix together the ingredients. When ready to serve we clip the bottom corner and squeeze the contents into each egg half! Clean up is just a toss and it looks very fancy!*

Lake Thomas BBQ Chicken

Lake Thomas is just outside of Gail, Texas in Borden County. My parents had an amazing BBQ grill made from an old oil drum cut in half. They had some of the most amazing parties at that lake! My father LOVED Texas and he was a Texas Caballero! He could lasso anything that did not move, he loved "Bourbon and Branch," listened to Western Music and survived rattlesnakes and getting stung by a scorpion! My Dad's chicken was famous for two things; 1) he always used Mesquite wood and 2) he always dropped a couple pieces in the sand!

This was his chicken recipe minus the sand!
3 whole chickens cut into serving pieces
1 stick butter
½ cup bourbon whiskey
1 cup ketchup
2 TB vinegar
1 tsp salt
¼ tsp pepper

¼ cup onion finely chopped
2 TB Worcestershire sauce
2 TB lemon juice
2 TB brown sugar
I tsp dry mustard powder

In a pot add butter and melt. Add onion and cook until soft but not brown. Now add the remaining ingredients and cook slowly until thick.

QUICK TIP This sauce can be made up to three days in advance.

There are two schools of thought on BBQ chicken one being that raw chicken must be slowly cooked on the BBQ and basted until cooked to perfection. Although we agree with this, when preparing chicken, there is nothing worse than a guest screaming in horror because they saw some blood near the bone and pushing their plate away and telling your guests what they saw on TV about chicken.

Here is a simple solution:

Place the chicken pieces in a large frying pan. Add water to almost cover the chicken and add 2 bouillon cubes, salt and pepper to taste. Bring contents to a boil. After about 15 minutes, check chicken by piercing it to see if the juices are clear. Remove from heat and let sit 15 minutes.

QUICK TIP You can prepare the chicken to this point and store in a container in the refrigerator adding in the liquid to the chicken.

When ready to BBQ, place chicken on grill with coals red/white hot. As the chicken skin begins to brown, baste with BBQ sauce. Turn chicken pieces to prevent burning. Should you get a burned spot immediately add BBQ sauce to the area. Continue basting, cooking and turning until the chicken is cooked (if you used the pre-cooked method, then cook until hot), coated with a nice glaze of BBQ sauce.

Tahoka Hwy Cole Slaw

When traveling through Texas there is a plethora of Truck Stops and Diners along the highway that serve this coleslaw. The coolness is a perfect balance to the spicy BBQ.

1 small head cabbage, shredded

1 or 2 carrots, peeled and shredded

1 small white onion, grated

½ cup buttermilk

¾ cup mayonnaise

2 TB white vinegar

1 tsp sugar

½ tsp salt

Shred cabbage into a large bowl. Add carrots and onion and toss together. Make dressing by mixing together buttermilk, mayonnaise, vinegar, sugar and salt. Toss it all together!

> **QUICK TIP** *Casa Cebadillas makes this salad the day before in a re-sealable plastic bag and when ready to serve we just empty the contents into a serving bowl.*

Baptist Potluck Potato Salad

10 large red skin potatoes

2 tsp salt

8 eggs, hard boiled, chopped

1½ cup mayonnaise (home-made is best)

¾ cup prepared mustard (regular yellow mustard)

¼ cup apple cider vinegar

2 large onions chopped

6 oz. chopped pimentos

1 tsp celery seed

14 to 16 oz. jar sweet or dill pickles, finely chopped (depending if you prefer a sweet or savory salad)

Boil potatoes with their jackets on until cooked through and can be pierced with a fork. Drain and cool completely. Mix mayonnaise, mustard, salt, celery seed and vinegar together and then add the chopped onions. Cut potatoes in half and the slice into ½ inch slices. Fold potatoes, egg and pimentos into the dressing. Chill for at least 3 hours.

King Ranch Cornbread

3 TB bacon drippings
2 eggs
1½ cup corn meal
1 tsp salt
½ tsp baking soda
1¼ cup buttermilk

Preheat oven to 400. In a cast-iron skillet, fry three pieces of bacon to get the drippings. Eat the bacon or make a BLT sandwich. In a mixing bowl beat eggs and add cornmeal, salt baking soda and buttermilk.

Pour this mixture into the hot cast-iron skillet with the bacon drippings and immediately place into the oven. Turn the heat down to 375. When it rises and starts to gets a few brown spots and when a knife inserted comes out clean it is ready to remove from the oven. Serve right from the pan with fresh butter.

Needless Mark-up Pralines

1 cup firmly packed light brown sugar
1 cup sugar
½ cup light cream
1 cup pecan halves
2 TB butter

Mix sugar and water together and cook until it reaches the soft ball stage. Add the cream and pecans. Stir. Remove from heat and working quickly, add the butter and stir again. Drop by tablespoonful portions onto wax paper. Cool and serve.

QUICK TIP Make these a day or two in advance and keep covered in an airtight container.

Alternatives to BBQ Chicken
Baby Back Ribs

2 racks of baby back ribs, 2 to 2½ lbs. each
2 TB olive oil
1 TB chili powder
2 tsp brown sugar
1½ tsp salt
1 tsp garlic powder
1 tsp sweet paprika
½ tsp ground cumin
½ tsp dried thyme
1 TB butter
1 TB garlic, minced or pressed
1 TB canned chipotle chilies with adobo sauce
2 TB light brown sugar
2 TB red wine vinegar
1 tsp Worcestershire sauce
¼ cup fresh orange juice
1 cup ketchup
1 TB molasses or miel de caña
Pre-boil ribs until cooked.

Mix the remaining ingredients into a pan and simmer until hot. Par-boil ribs for 30 minutes. Place on BBQ wrill with grey-white coals. Baste ribs on BBQ grill with this sauce until a nice coating is achieved. Serve extra sauce on the side.

SUPER EASY Cowboy Brisket

4 - 7 lbs. fresh cut beef brisket
3 cloves garlic slivered
3 cloves garlic crushed
4 large onions thinly sliced
1 cup apple cider vinegar
1½ TB bacon drippings
1 cup strong black coffee
Salt and pepper to taste
¾ cup bourbon
1 TB Liquid Smoke

Salt and pepper liberally, add brisket in a container or re-sealable plastic bag. Mix the garlic, onions, vinegar, drippings, coffee, liquid smoke and half cup bourbon. Take the remainder quarter cup bourbon and drink it to be sure everything is OK. Let the brisket marinate overnight. Let yourself marinate as well.

OVEN METHOD: The following day, place the brisket and marinade in a roasting pan. Add BBQ sauce to cover (recipe above). Cover with foil and roast at 300 degrees for 4 hours. Uncover and allow to rest in the warm oven for 30 minutes.

BBQ METHOD: Traditionally brisket is slow roasted for eight to ten hours on a low flame or after using about 20 pounds of charcoal! What we do is follow the oven method above, however do not add the BBQ sauce prior to slow roasting. After four hours, remove from oven and place brisket on a BBQ grill with white-gray coals and baste with BBQ sauce. Turn frequently and continue to mop BBQ sauce on both sides of brisket. Sauce will begin to caramelize and develop small charred marks. Once the entire brisket is covered in a nice BBQ sauce glaze remove and allow to rest 30 minutes before carving. Serve extra sauce on the side.

NOTE – Brisket of beef is a cut of beef taken from the breast section under the first five ribs. Brisket is usually sold without the bone and is divided into two sections. The flat cut has minimal fat and is usually more expensive than the more flavorful point cut, which has more fat. Briskets require long, slow cooking and are best when braised. Corned beef is made from brisket.`

Southern Sunday Dinner

Mint Julep or Nehi Cocktail

Classic bourbon cocktail or our adult version of this famous southern soda

Hot Jezebel

Hot artichoke parmesan spread

Zetha's Fried Chicken

Slightly spicy crisp fried chicken

Mashed Potatoes and Gravy

Freshly mashed potatoes with southern gravy

Coleslaw

Slightly sweet and savory coleslaw

Sister Hogg's Biscuits

Southern biscuits guaranteed not to get stuck in the squat!

Apple Pie a-la-mode

Fresh spiced apples in a flakey crust

Your dinner tonight will be reminiscent of a typical Southern after Church "Social." Of course no "spirits" were served while the preacher was around or occasionally it was disguised in lemonade or iced tea. Once I remember a spiked watermelon accidentally got sent to a table of preachers. What I hear is that not one said a word… but come to find out those preachers were all putting the seeds in their pockets! We all chuckled privately that the preacher was telling the congregation that everyone should get the "demon liquor" right now and pour it in the river. Then the next hymn played was "Shall We Gather at the River" and we all snickered and whispered "Yeah, downstream!"

Décor for this dinner can be elegant or "country" you can take it either direction. At Casa Cebadillas we go for a Southern Supper with white tablecloth, china and crystal which is a great contrast to the cuisine. We play gospel hymns in the background; we have a bible on the table and make fake labels on the liquor bottles "just in case the preacher man comes!"

Southern Sunday Dinner Recipes:

Nehi Cocktail

At Lake Thomas we would scour the cabin looking in the cushions of every chair to come up with the 15 cents it would take to go to Lem's Marina and buy a NeHi Grape Soda. This is our adult version of this classic drink!

2 oz. vodka

1 oz. raspberry liqueur

3 oz. sweet-n-sour mix (see recipe page …)

Place all ingredients in a martini shaker and shake well. Pour into an ice filled hurricane glass, top with a splash of soda and garnish with a lemon.

Mint Julep

If you have Mint Julep cups and sippers this is perfect. If my mom is reading this and wonders why some of hers were missing, well as a kid the metal cups made perfect molds for making castles in the sand-box at the park which I forgot to return home and have not confessed this until now (sorry Mom).

The basics of a Mint Julep:

Get a double old fashion glass and place a teaspoon of confectioners sugar and a sprig of mint and muddle until bruised well (not you but the mint). Now add a layer of crushed ice and another spoon of sugar and mint and muddle again. Repeat this process one more time until you have completed three layers. Now get a quarter cup (two ounces) of bourbon and pour on top. As the bourbon travels down through the layers, it will melt the ice and mix with the mint and sugar. Take a straw and place to the bottom of the glass. Now sip slowly this cool drink and have visions of Rhett Butler and Scarlet O'hara

Hot Jezebel

1 eight oz. pkg cream cheese
1 cup shredded parmesan cheese
1 cup shredded mozzarella cheese
¼ cup chopped parsley
1 twenty-four oz. can artichoke hearts
1 seven oz. jar roasted red peppers, drained and chopped
1 pkg crackers (plain water cracker)

Pre-heat the oven to 400 degrees. Place all ingredients except the red pepper in a food processor. Pulse until blended. Add red pepper and pulse again until peppers are incorporated but still in pieces. Place this mixture into an ovenproof container that you will use to serve. Bake until bubbling. Remove and let cool slightly, bring to the table with crackers and a spreading knife.

Zetha's Fried Chicken with Country Gravy

As a child I was fascinated watching Zetha make her prized Fried Chicken. She would test the oil by dipping her fingers into water and "baptizing" the grease and when it splattered from the water it was time for the chicken. She took such care placing each piece while singing gospel hymns.

Dry Mix:
3 cups all-purpose flour
1½ TB garlic salt
1 TB ground black pepper
1 TB paprika
½ tsp poultry seasoning
½ tsp salt
Batter:
1 1/3 cup all-purpose flour
1 tsp salt
¼ tsp ground black pepper
2 egg yolks, beaten
1½ cup beer
Preparation:
1 qt. vegetable oil for frying
3 whole chickens, cut into pieces

Heat oil until it sizzles when you "baptize" with a little water (350 degrees). A cast-iron skillet is preferred or you can use a deep fat fryer. To get truly golden-brown and crispy chicken, you'll need a cast iron skillet. Cast iron is the best for even heat distribution and temperature maintenance. Roll each piece of chicken in the dry mix, then into the batter and then back into the dry mix and then into the pan. Fry in batches since overcrowding the pan will lower the temperature of the oil dramatically, causing more oil to be absorbed and resulting in soggy, greasy, gross chicken. When the chicken pieces are deep golden brown, remove from the pan and transfer to a cooling rack set over a baking sheet to catch any drips. Insert an instant-read thermometer into the chicken to make sure it is fully cooked before proceeding with the next batch. Fried chicken is best served immediately. However, you can keep warm in the oven but you run a risk of the crust becoming soggy.

Gravy

Traditionally, the grease is poured off from the cast-iron pot after cooking meat and flour is added and heated to form a roux. Then milk, salt and pepper are added and it forms what is known as "country gravy." I still remember the first time I was introduced to this gravy. It was the first time I spent the night at someone else's home. In the morning, my friend Kenneth asked his Mom if we could have Biscuits and Gravy for breakfast. I still remember watching his mother take the used grease from the night before out of a can with a strainer lid and proceeded to make this gravy. I had no idea how to eat this plate of paste and bread and was horrified that people actually ate it. It is the preferred gravy on Chicken Fried stead in the South. As you may have gathered I am not preparing this gravy since I do not feel it compliments the mashed potatoes.

In a frying pan, add equal parts flour and butter and stir with a wooden spoon over medium heat until the roux is golden. Now add a strong chicken broth until you achieve the desired thickness. Add salt and fresh cracked pepper to taste.

Mashed Potatoes

6 potatoes
Salt and pepper to taste
1 cup sour cream
1 stick butter

Peel and quarter potatoes. Boil until a knife is easily inserted into the quarters. Add butter and sour cream in a microwavable container and heat until butter is melted. Drain potatoes and place quarters in a potato ricer in batches, back into the hot pot. Now add the melted butter/sour cream mixture and sprinkle with salt and pepper to taste (about 2 healthy pinches, guests can always add more). Take a wire whisk and beat until smooth and cover until ready to serve. Do not over beat.

Cole Slaw

5 cups chopped cabbage
½ cup chopped curly parsley tops
¼ cup chopped green onion
¼ tsp salt
Dressing:
½ cup sour cream
¼ cup mayonnaise
1 TB honey mustard
1½ tsp white vinegar
½ tsp sugar
¼ tsp sal

Place cabbage, parsley, green onion and salt in a bowl. In a separate container, mix the dressing and fold the dressing into the cabbage mixture. Refrigerate at least one hour before serving.

Sister Hogg's Biscuits

I remember the first time Zetha let me try to make biscuits. They did not rise! I was upset and she gave me a hug and said, "LORDY child, they just got stuck in the squat!" She shared Sister Hogg's recipe with me and said their claim to fame was: Guaranteed not to get stuck in the squat!
2 cups all-purpose flour
1 TB baking powder
1 tsp salt
1 TB white sugar
1/3 cup shortening (equal parts butter and lard)
1 cup milk

Preheat oven to 375. Stir together flour, salt, baking powder and sugar. Add shortening and cut with a pastry cutter until the mixture resembles a coarse meal. Add milk and blend quickly until it forms a dough. DO NOT OVERWORK. Form dough into a rectangle and cut into serving pieces and place on a cookie sheet. Bake until they rise and brown on top. Serve hot with butter.

Apple Pie a-la-Mode

Crust: Makes one 9 inch double crust
1 9 inch pie tin
2 cups all purpose flour
1 tsp salt
2/3 cup shortening (equal parts lard and butter is best)
1 tsp vinegar
5 to 8 tsp milk

Preheat oven to 350 degrees. Combine flour and salt, cut in shortening with pastry blender until dough looks like peas. Add vinegar and enough milk to hold dough together. Make two balls out of the dough. Place dough in the refrigerator to rest for 30 minutes.

Roll out dough on well floured surface with a floured rolling pin. Put one crust in pie tin; trim dough edges equal to the pie tin edge.

Filling:
8 cups peeled sliced apples such as McIntosh or Granny Smith
½ cup sugar
1 TB cinnamon
1 TB butter
1 TB flour
¼ cup raisins
¼ cup dark spiced rum
1 egg white

Soak raisins overnight in rum. Place apples, cinnamon, flour and raisins in a large mixing bowl and stir to combine. Place the mixture in the pie tin. Sprinkle more cinnamon on top of apple mixture and dot with pieces of butter. Cover with the remaining pie crust, seal edges and flute, be sure to cut some slits (air holes) on this top crust. Beat egg white with a fork and brush on top of pie crust. Sprinkle with a pinch of sugar. Bake for 50 minutes to 1 hour depending on how brown you like the crust.

P.S. If you peel apples ahead of time. Put in a bowl with water and lemon so they don't turn brown.

Montmartre

Classic Champagne Cocktail

Amuse-bouche
Crevette cuite à la vapeur sur la mer verte

Amusee of Shrimp in a green goddess sea

Hors D'oeuvres
Pâté de foie poulet, Brie avec le tapenade de figue

Homemade Pate and small toasts with brie and fig tapenade

Salade
à l'endive Belge avec du fromage bleu et des noix de pécan

Endive salad with blue cheese and toasted pecans

Plat Principal
Canard à l'orange, petit pois de campagne, purée de pommes de terre
avec du beurre de truffe Ou riz sauvage

Orange duck served with country peas and mashed potatoes or Wild Rice

Dessert
mousse au chocolat

Chocolate Mousse

The theme for this particular dinner takes me back to a when I was a young adult. My parents took me to a very famous restaurant in Paris that is known for duck preparation. Each duck that is served is numbered and at the end of the meal you are presented a card with that particular duck's number I guess you could say that ducks number was up! My grandparents had taken my parents to this same restaurant. This restaurant is noted for the discovery of the fork and there was actually a duel to the death of one just for reservation.

Montmartre Recipes:

Classic Champagne Cocktail

6 brown or white sugar cubes
Angostura bitters
6 TB brandy
1 bottle chilled champagne

Preparation: Take a sugar cube and place it on the end of the bottle of the bitters. Turn the bottle upside down holding the sugar cube over the opening. Shake until the sugar cube changes color from saturation with bitters. Place cube in champagne flute and add one tablespoon brandy. Add champagne and serve.

Amusee Crevette cuite à la vapeur sur la mer verte

1 cup regular mayonnaise
1 cup (bunch) parsley
½ cup fresh tarragon leaves or 2 TB dried
1 bunch green onions including green tops
1 TB tarragon vinegar
1 can (2 oz.) anchovies, drained
6 Large Shrimp, cooked, cleaned and de-veined

Mix all the ingredients except the shrimp into a blender. Blend until smooth.

Cook shrimp by plunging in 1 quarts boiling water that you have added a TB crab boil or substitute 3 Bay leaves, teaspoon sage and 2 teaspoons salt. Clean and peel shrimp and chill until serving time.

To serve, we use a Chinese soup spoon and place a tablespoon of dressing on the bottom, the chilled shrimp on top and garnish with a tarragon leaf.

Pâté de foie Poulet

½ lb. liver
I medium onion
¼ mushrooms
I stick butter
½ cup maderia or cognac,
¼ cup sherry

Melt butter in frying pan on medium high heat, add onions and sauté until soft. Add livers and toss in melted butter until the livers turn gray, then add cognac or Maderia and flame. Simmer slowly until the livers are completely cooked and brown approximately 30 minutes. Add salt and pepper. Set aside to cool. In a jar blender add sherry then add the contents of the pan. Blend until smooth. While still warm, put pate into either a crock or into a greased silicon mold. If you use a crock, you can add beef aspic flavored with Maderia or port and ganrish with truffle slices on top.

QUICK TIP This freezes really well. If you use a silicon mold, remove while frozen, place in refrigerator unmolded and allow to thaw.

Although, you can use a plain water cracker with this, my favorite is to serve this pate with a kumquat quince paste on a pear cracker. The Pear cracker is really easy to make.

Pear Crackers (yield) 15 crackers

½ cup all-purpose flour
Scant pinch of salt
Scant pinch of baking soda
1½ TB butter softened
½ TB honey
½ TB warm water
3 TB pureed pear

Preheat the oven to 350. Combine the flour, salt, and baking soda in a large bowl or in the food processor. Cut in the butter until the mixture resembles coarse meal. Add pear and blend well.

In a separate bowl, dissolve the honey in the warm water. Slowly add the sweetened water to the flour-pear mixture and blend to form a dough that will hold together in a cohesive ball.

On a floured surface or pastry cloth, roll thin, at most an eighth of an inch. Cut into rectangles. Do not worry if they are uneven, this will enhance the rustic charm. Place on a lightly greased cookie sheet or parchment-lined baking sheet. Prick each cracker in two or three places with the tines of a fork. Bake for 15 to 20 minutes turning over once during baking, the crackers should be medium brown. Cool on a rack.

Brie avec le tapenade de figue

½ cup chopped dried figs
¼ cup warm water
½ cup chopped kalamata olives
½ TB olive oil
1 TB balsamic vinegar
1 clove garlic minced
½ tsp dried rosemary
½ tsp dried thyme
Scant tsp cayenne pepper
Salt and pepper to taste
1/8 cup chopped toasted walnuts

Place chopped figs in a bowl with the water and allow to soak for 1 hour. In a jar blender or food processor add all ingredients except the walnuts. Pulse until blended. Add walnuts and pulse again until incorporated and resembles a tapenade.

To serve, place on a mini toast point add a slice of brie and top with a teaspoon of tapenade.

Salade - à l'endive Belge avec du fromage bleu et des noix de pécan

Belgium endive, 3 heads
1 bag of pre-washed wild salad greens
1 wedge gorgonzola cheese 250 grams (try to select one with quite a few blue veins)
1 leek sliced in rings
½ cup toasted pecans
3 slices bacon cooked crisp
1/3 cup olive oil
1/3 cup sherry vinegar
12 grape tomatoes
Cracked pepper

On chilled salad plates place a small handful of wild greens. Arrange endive spears to fan out from the plate. Crumble blue cheese on top. Now place leek rings and pecans. Shake or blend oil and Sherry Vinegar and sprinkle on top of each salad. Garnish with 2 grape tomatoes, crumbles of bacon and fresh cracked pepper.

Canard à l'orange

6 Duck breasts
1 qt orange juice
Cointreau
Stock: pigeons, celery, onion, carrot, parsley
1 bottle red wine
¼ cup red wine vinegar
3 TB sugar
2 TB arrowroot
2 TB port wine
1 can (4 oz.) mandarin orange slices
Zest in strips of one orange

If you are able to purchase duck breasts this is the best. If not, purchase 2 ducks to yield eight servings. Remove duck wing ends, neck and giblets and cut duck into four serving pieces. Ask your butcher if you can order duck breasts which is much easier.

In a sealable bag add duck and equal parts wine and orange juice. You will most likely need two bags. You need to let this marinate for a minimum of 24 hours.

Using a zester, make long strips of orange peel. Place peel in a small saucepan of cold water and bring to a boil. Drain. Fill with cold water and bring to a boil again. Repeat this process for a total of three boils. This is to remove the bitterness of the zest. For the fourth boil, add ½ cup water and ¼ cup sugar and boil until the zest begins to resemble orange string. Remove from heat and place on wax paper to cool. These will be used to garnish the duck.

Make stock.

In Spain quail and pigeon are readily available and inexpensive otherwise use the duck wings or substitute chicken wings. If you use chicken, you will need to supplement your stock with a bit of beef demi-glace or even add some veal stock.

Brown your bird of choice in a 400 degree oven along with a stalk of celery, a quartered onion and a thickly sliced carrot. Shake and toss until vegetables are becoming brown. Add this entire mixture into a stock-pot and add stock or water to cover and four parsley sprigs and a bay leaf. Bring to a simmer and skim off foam. Simmer for three hours. Remove from heat and strain off all fat. Return to pot and boil down until you have two cups of stock.

To Prepare:
Remove duck breast from bags and save marinade. In a sauce pan, add stock and bring to a boil. Add marinade and boil to reduce.

Place breasts skin side up in a broiler pan with sides at least one inch tall. Prick breasts all over with a fork and salt and pepper each piece. Pre heat oven broiler.

Place duck under broiler and begin making the sauce right away.

Keep your eye on the duck because you do not want it to over crisp or burn. As it cooks, using a bulb baster to remove excess fat. The breasts are done when the juices are rosy when pricked. Remember the duck will continue to cook after removing from the broiler, so do not wait until the juices are clear. If duck is done too soon, place in the oven on the bottom rack to stay warm away from the heating element.

Sauce:
In a large frying pan add the three tablespoons of sugar and vinegar. Boil rapidly and caramelize until it is dark brown. Remove from heat and add half the stock stirring to dissolve all the mixture and return to heat. When bubbling again remove from heat and add the remaining stock and arrowroot, return to the stove and simmer on low heat until the sauce is thickened. Add the drained mandarin orange slices, ½ cup dry port and ¼ cup Cointreau, stir on low until steam rises. Remove from heat and add 2 tablespoons butter and mix with a wire whisk to incorporate.

Serve:
Place duck breast on plate and spoon sauce over, garnish with candied zest. Serve with Wild Rice or Mashed Potatoes.

Riz Sauvage

I prefer wild rice with this dish however we found many Europeans were not familiar with wild rice. Often we were asked if they could try the wild rice so we began offering both. I feel the duck requires simple accompaniments. Because of this, at Casa Cebadillas, the side dishes are presented in the middle of the table to be shared.

Wild rice is often available in the store mixed with other rice. We prefer pure 100% wild rice and not a combination.

2 cups wild rice
3 cups beef stock
1 small chopped onion
1 TB butter
Pinch salt

Rinse wild rice three times changing the water each time. In a saucepan, sauté butter and onion until onion is soft. Add rice and toss to coat. Add beef broth and bring to a boil. Cover tightly.

Reduce heat to low and cook for 30 to 45 minutes until the rice grains begins to split. Remove cover and fluff with fork.

> *NOTE – If your pan does not have a tight cover, place foil on top first then the cover to assure a good seal and steam (caution, the foil will become hot).*

Petit Pois de campagne

4 slices of bacon
½ stick butter
1 small bunch green onion, chopped including some of the green parts
4 to 6 leaves of Boston Bibb lettuce sliced chiffonade
1 small can of peas
1 32 oz. bag of frozen peas (if you can get fresh peas this is ideal)

In a frying pan, sauté the bacon until thoroughly cooked but not crisp. Add butter and continue to sauté. Add onion and only the juice from the can of peas. Bring to a simmer and add the chiffonade lettuce. Add this sauce to the heated or steamed peas.

> *QUICK TIP The Sauce for the peas can be made the day before and stored in the refrigerator. When you are ready to serve, heat the sauce in the microwave until bubbling. In another container, heat the frozen peas until hot but not to the point they begin to shrivel. When they are hot, add the hot sauce and toss together.*

Purée de pommes

6 peeled potatoes quartered
8 oz. creme fraiche or sour cream
1 stick butter
1 coarsely chopped truffle (optional but really good)

Boil potatoes until you can pierce with a fork. Drain. Use a potato ricer and rice them back into the hot pan. Microwave ½ stick butter and crème fraiche until melted. Sprinkle potatoes with three healthy pinches of salt and two dashes of white pepper. Add hot crème butter mixture and whip with wire whisk until incorporated. Do not over whip. Taste and correct for salt. Remember, it is better to under salt and have extra at the table.

While potatoes are boiling, mix other ½ stick butter with coarsely chopped truffle until completely incorporated. Place in wax paper, roll into a log and refrigerate.

To serve: Remove truffle butter from refrigerator and wax paper and cut into six pieces. Place kitchen spoonful of mashed potato on plate and top with a round of truffle butter.

Dessert Mousse de chocolat (Home-made Chocolate Mousse)

With this dessert, I cheat! I admit I do not make a classic mousse but by the time I have done everything else on this dinner I feel I can fudge a little on a chocolate dessert. Also, this dinner is heavy and this mousse is a lighter version. You can also modify this recipe and put into an ice-cream maker and make a wonderful Chocolate Mousse Ice-Cream!

I½ cups heavy cream
1/8 tsp vanilla extract
6 oz. bitter dark chocolate chopped
I TB butter
I TB sugar
I TB espresso or strong coffee
2 oz. liqueur of coffee, orange, mint or raspberry

In a large sauce pan, add chocolate, butter and sugar and place on low heat until melted. Remove from heat and add liqueur of your choice stirring constantly until incorporated. If it begins to congeal, return to stove but only allow it to become warm.

In a chilled metal bowl, whip cream and vanilla until the cream holds it shape. Take a large spoonful of whipped cream and add to the saucepan with chocolate sauce. Fold together. With a rubber spatula, fold this chocolate cream into the large container of whipped cream. Fold until incorporated but do not over-fold. Place into individual dessert glasses or even wine glasses. We find it easier to place mousse into pastry bag and pipe into serving dishes. Cover and chill immediately.

NOTE — my Dad called me and asked if he could just buy some pudding mix, throw some liquor in it and mix it with a canister of whipped topping. After my moment of complete horror I decided to calmly explain why this should not be done. A true mousse involves pure chocolate, sugar and egg yolks incorporated with egg whites. My recipe eliminates the eggs and uses cream instead. The whipped topping he was referring to is actually a petroleum based product and the pudding mix is far from a dense chocolate base. One should never declare a mousse using my father's shortcut.

Polynesian Luau

Mai Tai Cocktail with a Lei Greeting

Rum and fruit juice cocktail and a traditional Hawaiian greeting!

Pu Pu Platter

Starter platter of Crab Rangoon, Coconut Shrimp,
Huli Huli Chicken and Rumaki
Crab and cream cheese in a Wonton wrapper with
Chinese Hot Mustard Dipping Sauce
Coconut Crusted Shrimp served with Sweet Chili Sauce
Charcoal Grilled Chicken Legs with Teriyaki BBQ Sauce
Dates stuffed with Marinated Chicken Livers and wrapped in bacon

Hukilau Fruit Platter

Platter of fresh tropical fruit sprinkled with date sugar and rum

Kalua Pig
with Hawaiian Slaw and Jasmine Rice

Pork Leg with dry rub of spices, wrapped in banana leaves and slow roasted in an
earth oven served with a Napa Cabbage and Pineapple Slaw
and Jasmine Rice

Coconut Ice-cream

Coconut Ice-cream served in a Coconut shell

Kilauea Eruption

This communal dessert is a large brownie volcano, surrounding an
ice-cream core with raspberry lava, candy boulders and showers of sparks! Great for Birthdays and Celebrations

My mother was an amazing cook and host. At a very early age I was taught that the number one concern is your guests comfort and enjoyment. She was the "Queen" of themed parties and I give her tremendous credit for the ideas and themes at Casa Cebadillas. Never will I forget her infamous Luau complete with grass skirted clad warriors with spears guiding guests to the backyard where they were greeted with a fresh lei, listening to Hawaiian music, suckling pigs, Mai-Tais and more. To this day she still gives an amazing party! Recently for my father's 90th Birthday she hosted a Spanish themed extravaganza with Matadors and invitations exclaiming 90 – NO BULL! I also was blessed with a father who loves to cook and is very creative. He has created some amazing meals from ingredients I never thought would work. When I go home to visit, a requirement I have is for his Seafood Lasagna. Anyone who has attended a party at their house will agree that they are both fantastic hosts.

MAI TAI

2 oz. light rum
2 oz. orange juice
2 oz. pineapple juice
1 oz. dark rum
½ oz. crème de noyeaux

In a hurricane glass fill with ice and add light rum, orange juice and pineapple juice. Garnish with wedges of pineapple and lime speared on a toothpick. Then float the dark rum over the top of the drink and drizzle with crème de noyeaux.

QUICK TIP You can pre-make the main part of this drink by combining the light rum and juices together in a pitcher and place in the refrigerator until ready to serve. When your guests arrive all you need to do is pour the juice mixture, garnish and float the dark rum and crème de noyeaux.

Crab Rangoon

½ lb. fresh crabmeat drained and chopped
½ lb. cream cheese
½ tsp steak sauce (like HP® or A-I®)
1 crushed clove of garlic or ¼ tsp powdered garlic
18 wonton wrappers
1 egg yolk beaten
Oil for frying (deep fat fryer is best)

Mix crab, cream cheese, steak sauce and garlic together. Place a teaspoon of crab in the middle of the wonton. Brush egg yolk around the edges and gather together to form a purse. Drop into hot oil and fry until crispy. Drain on paper towels.

Serve hot with sides of chinese hot mustard, chinese red sauce and pineapple chili sauces for dipping.

Rumaki

¼ lb. chicken livers trimmed and rinsed
¼ cup soy sauce
1 TB finely grated peeled fresh ginger
2 TB packed light brown sugar
½ tsp curry powder
1 lb. bacon

1 can water chestnuts each sliced in half horizontally

Mix soy, ginger, sugar and curry together. Set aside. Cut trimmed livers to serving sizes. One liver will make approximately two to three serving pieces. Add livers to sauce and toss. Take bacon strips and cut in half. Now cut this half into two long pieces. Place a piece of bacon in front of you. At the top end, add a water chestnut and a piece of liver. Roll towards you and then secure with a toothpick. Place on a cookie sheet or broiler pan and put under a pre-heated 500° broiler. Watch carefully that the toothpicks don't burn too much. With tongs turn pieces over to assure the bacon is cooked on both sides. Once they are cooked completely, keep warm and serve immediately.

QUICK TIP We make these the day before and store them in the refrigerator in their marinade and take them out when we are ready to bake

Angel's On Horseback

Our version which there are several! You can also use scallops in place of the water chestnuts for your "angels."

Get whole dates and remove the pits.
Stuff date with a water chestnut piece.
Wrap with bacon and broil the same as the rumaki.

Coconut Shrimp

Practice being modest when you receive numerous compliments for this dish, it is really a winner!

18 raw shrimp cleaned, shelled and deveined.
Batter:
½ cup all-purpose flour
½ cup cornstarch

½ TB white pepper
I TB olive oil
I tsp salt
I cup ice water
2 cups shredded coconut
Sauce:
½ cup orange marmalade
¼ cup Dijon country mustard (with seeds)
¼ cup honey
3 dashes hot chili sauce like Tabasco®

For batter, mix dry ingredients in a bowl. Add oil and water to dry ingredients and stir to blend. Heat oil in a deep frying pan (deep fat fryer is best yet again... maybe you should just go get one) to at least 350 degrees. Dip shrimp in batter and roll in coconut. Place in fryer and fry until lightly brown. If you broke down and bought that deep fryer this would take about 2 minutes. If you are cooking in a frying pan it may be 4 minutes. Do not overcook.

Mix sauce ingredients together and serve with the shrimp. Sauce can be made up to two days in advance.

Chicken Huli Huli

18 chicken wings, each cut into serving pieces at the joint. Each chicken wing should have the part with the wing tip removed. You want them to be almost like miniature drumsticks. If you are unable to get wings, reduce to 6 drum sticks but they can be awkward to eat with your hands.

BBQ Sauce:
I/3 cup ketchup
½ cup brown sugar
3 TB sherry
I to 3 inch piece ginger root shredded
I clove of garlic minced

Mix together and cook on the stove top until hot. Remove from heat.

On a BBQ grill with hot coals place the chicken, turning to heat through. Baste with sauce and continue to turn and baste until hot, glazed and brown. Serve immediately.

> **QUICK TIP** *Nothing changes the mood of a party than the sight of undercooked chicken. We have found to eliminate doubts, do the following: In a large frying pan place chicken pieces, add chicken broth, five pepper corns and one tsp of ginger. Boil until chicken is done. You will see blood appear near the bone when it is close to being done. Remove from heat and let sit for 10 minutes. Place in a container and cover with a small amount of cooled cooking liquid until cool and then refrigerate. This can be done the day before.*

> *NOTE — since guests are using fingers, a quick clean up are moist towelettes. We use packaged Baby Wipes, remove enough for the guests, place in bowl, squeeze a wedge of lemon over them and microwave for 30 seconds, the warm towelette is a nice touch and offers a perfect clean-up at the end of the pu-pu course.*

Tropical Fruit Platter

Our centerpiece is usually fresh seasonal tropical fruit. After guests have had their pu-pu platter, we have them to come to the table by offering a tray of fruit to be consumed communally. We simply remove the centerpiece and cut up the fruit and present it back to the table with tooth picks. We do enhance some of the fruit; example, we peel back a banana leaving the peel but cut in thick slices and sprinkle with date sugar and rum, papaya is sliced and a squeeze of lime is added to cut the sweetness.

Kalua Pig

Purchase a whole pig shoulder, gauging about ½ pound per person. If you are unable to get this, ask your butcher for six pig knuckles. If this is still a challenge you can use a pork butt but it will not be as tender.

Use a large casserole earthen pot that will hold the entire pork. There are many clay cookers on the market and anyone of them will work as long as it will accommodate your pork. Many of you probably have one of these clay cookers and never thought you would really need it. Well go to your storage closet and get it out because it is perfect for this!

Rub pork with a full tablespoon of kosher salt. We use Brittany sea salt. Give a few turns of fresh cracked pepper. Now add two tablespoons liquid smoke. Wrap Pork with a banana leaf * and place in clay cooker. Be sure the top is completely sealed to keep the steam inside. Place in a cold oven six hours before serving time. Turn oven on to 350 degrees, after two hours reduce the heat to 300, then after 4 hours reduce the heat to 200. 30 minutes before you want to serve, remove from oven but do not take the top off. The end result will be a soft favorable pork with a wonderful sauce.

* Banana leaves are often available in ethnic markets in the frozen section. We have found them in many Latin and Asian stores. In the event you cannot find them anywhere, you can use spinach leaves, the effect will not be the same, but it will be acceptable. Use an entire bag of fresh whole spinach leaves.

Jasmine Rice

Prepare rice as package indicates.
We are convinced jasmine rice must be available everywhere if we can find it in our tiny village!

Hawaiian Slaw

Slice thinly one small head of Napa cabbage after removing the core. Toss with ¼ cup rice vinegar, one tablespoon sesame oil and mandarin orange slices or pineapple pieces. Garnish with toasted sesame seeds.

Coconut Ice-Cream

4 oz. sugar
4 egg yolks
½ pint milk
½ pint double cream
½ tsp pure vanilla extract
3 oz. cream of coconut

In a saucepan heat the milk to the boiling point and remove from heat. Beat sugar and egg yolks together then pour into milk and stir constantly with a wooden spoon over low heat until the custard coats the back of the spoon. Remove from heat and add coconut cream. Cool completely and proceed with your ice-cream maker's manufacture instructions.

Volcano Eruption Cake

Brownie Mountain:
1 cup butter, melted
3 cups white sugar
1 TB vanilla extract
4 eggs
1½ cups all-purpose flour
1 cup unsweetened cocoa powder
1 tsp salt
1 cup semisweet chocolate chips
Marshmallow crème

Raspberry Jam
Candy bars
I qt ice-cream any flavor
Sparklers

DIRECTIONS

Preheat oven to 350, lightly grease a cookie sheet or line with parchment paper.

Combine the melted butter, sugar, and vanilla in a large bowl. Beat in the eggs, one at a time, mixing well after each until thoroughly blended. Sift together the flour, cocoa powder and salt. Gradually stir the flour mixture into the chocolate mixture until blended. Stir in the chocolate morsels. Spread the batter evenly into the prepared baking dish.

Bake in preheated oven until an inserted toothpick comes out clean, 35 to 40 minutes. Remove from oven, and cool completely before cutting. Cut the brownie in half and then cut each of the halves from the top corner to the bottom corner forming two triangles, you will have a total of four triangles. Cut the tip of each triangle to make an area for "lava" to come out.

Lava:
Mix marshmallow cream and raspberry jam until you achieve the desired color and yet, the lava is thick.

Candy Boulders:
Have a bowl of chocolate covered peanuts or broken candy bars for your "rocks."

Assembly:
Unmold entire quart of ice-cream onto a serving tray. Quickly, lean the four brownie sides against the ice-cream. Toss rocks and sprinkle "cocoa" dirt on mountain. Spoon lava on top and allow it to drip down. Light sparklers and present to the table.

Depending on the size of pan you use for the brownie you may have to use a quart and a pint of ice-cream, one on top of the other, to achieve the height of the brownie.

Photo by Miro Slav OtraVista Photography, España

Ciao Bella

Sgroppino Cocktail
Lemon scented and Vodka infused Champagne

Amuse-bouche
Frittata freddo della cipolla con il caviale
Small egg onion cold frittata with caviar

Antipasti de Olivas della Casa, Patatine del Parmigiano,
Our Own Citrus Marinated Olives, Parmesan Crisps

Insalata Arrostita della Pera
Roasted Pears with Gorgonzola Cheese on Rocket Lettuce with a sherry vinaigrette

Osso Bucco
Veal "slow roasted campagna" style with fresh gremolata garnish

Patate del Aglio Arrostite
Roasted Garlic Potatoes

Nubi di Cielo
*Mostachones soaked in rum and layered with
turron ice-cream and chocolate*

Osso Bucco has to be my absolute favorite dish! I still remember my first experience having this wonderful slow roasted veal. It was in a typical dark wood panel leather holster booth Italian restaurant. As a child, I recall the waiter providing a small knife with the dish. He explained this knife was to extract the marrow from the bone. Once in Spain, we ordered this cut of meat by carefully providing illustrations of the calf and showing exactly where the cuts should be taken from. The butcher was delighted to present to us the following day our cuts of meat. But butcher proudly exclaimed that they had carefully removed the bone. I did not have the heart to tell the butcher that it is the bone that makes this Osso Bucco.

Décor for this theme has so many possibilities. You can make it as elegant or as simple as you desire. Once, on a beautiful summer evening in Seattle, I took all my formal dining room furniture out onto the lawn outside and served this meal "al fresco". Serve rustic bread and a nice wine and who could complain?

Ciao Bella Recipes

Sgroppino Cocktail

1 bottle chilled Prosecco (Italian sparkling white wine)
6 TB chilled vodka
2/3 cup frozen lemon sorbet
½ tsp chopped fresh mint leaves

Allow the sorbet to thaw enough to stir in the vodka and chopped mint and return to freezer until ready to serve.

In each champagne glass place a tablespoon of the sorbet mixture. Top with Prosecco and serve.

Frittata freddo della cipolla con il caviale

3 green onions or ½ spring onion
3 hard boiled eggs
3 TB unsalted butter
I TB Sour Cream/Crème Fraiche (save remainder for dessert)
Caviar
Fresh dill sprigs

Chop the onion including a little of the green into small pieces. In a saucepan, melt butter and add onion only to soften. Remove from heat. Chop hard boiled eggs and stir into onion butter mixture. In a three by nine inch bread pan, brush with butter. Now line with plastic wrap and assure that the inside is incased in plastic. Spoon the egg/onion mixture into the prepared pan and refrigerate until completely cooled.

To serve: Unmold chilled egg/onion mixture. Cut carefully into 6 portions and place on individual serving plates. Place a teaspoon of crème fraiche on each frittata. Now place a ½ teaspoon of caviar on top of this and garnish with a small sprig of dill. Serve immediately.

Olivas Arturo

¾ cup kalamata olives (with pits)
¾ cup cracked brine-cured Spanish Olives (with pits)
½ cup olive oil
¼ cup cilantro
2 TB or juice of ½ lemon
2 TB or juice of ½ orange
3 large garlic cloves sliced thinly
1½ TB fresh chopped parsley
½ TB grated lemon peel
½ TB grated orange peel
¼ teaspoon dried crushed red pepper

Place the olives in separate containers and cover with water, let stand overnight (12 to 24 hours), changing the water at least once. This procedure helps extract the salt from the commercial brine the olives were packaged in. Allow to drain thoroughly.

In a large olive jar at least 16 oz. place the olives, and all remaining ingredients. Seal tightly and rotate until all olives have been coated completely. Store in a cool area, turning upside down twice a day, I usually place the jar inside an empty storage container to capture any leakage should the seal not be tight enough. This recipe should be made at least three days in advance to allow all the flavors to meld; I usually begin the process one week in advance of the dinner.

Parmesan Crisps

8 oz. wedge parmesan cheese, hand grated.

Preheat oven to 350. Prepare a cookie sheet by lining with a silicon baking matt. Place a table-spoon of cheese per serving on the matt, leaving space to allow the cheese to melt.

Bake until they are bubbling and turning brown. Remove from oven allow to cool. Store carefully since they are very fragile. We place in a food container lined with paper towels until ready to serve, they can be made one day in advance.

Roasted Pear Salad

I Tb butter
I TB honey
1/8 cinnamon
3 or 4 pears
2 TB dry sherry
2 TB white wine vinegar
I TB olive oil
Walnuts
Serrano ham
Gorgonzola
Wild greens
Pre-heat oven to 500.

Slice and core pears and cut into larger bite sized chunks (they will shrink in the oven). Place the pears in a small shallow roasting pan. Add butter, honey and cinnamon and roast pears for 20 minutes. Remove from hot oven. Add to the accumulated juices at the bottom of the pan, dry sherry white wine vinegar and olive oil.

In a small frying pan add Serrano ham and sauté until crispy. Set aside until serving.

To serve salad: On each salad plate place a handful of wild greens and equally distribute roasted pear, walnuts, Serrano ham and chunks of gorgonzola. Drizzle warm dressing over salad.

Osso Bucco

2 TB butter
2 TB olive oil
I onion slivered
I leek cut into rounds
Garlic
Salt and pepper
4 TB flour
6 shanks with the bone please
I TB tomato paste
Veal Stock (1/2 beef and ½ Chicken)
½ Bottle red or white wine

Gremolata:
1 TB fresh parsley,
1 clove garlic crushed
3 Tb butter
Grated zest of one lemon.

In a heavy casserole, place butter and olive oil and heat until close to smoking point. Dredge Osso Bucco in flour, salt and pepper. Brown Osso Bucco on both sides and then remove from casserole. Add onion and leek and sauté until soft. There should be brown bits on the bottom of the casserole. Deglaze with wine. Return Osso Bucco to casserole and add stock until the liquid is half way up the thickness of the meat. Cover and simmer on low on the stove top or in a 300 degree oven for 3 hours.

Remove cover and baste with juices. Add tomato paste into sauce. Return to oven or stove top for 15 minutes.

Mix gremolata together until it forms a paste. Divide into 6 portions.

To serve, place Osso Bucco on plate, add some sauce and top with the gremolata. You can also garnish with a sprig of rosemary in the bone for a bit of drama.

Roasted Garlic Potatoes

1 large potato per person
1 whole head garlic roasted*
Chicken Broth
8 oz. sour cream
1 stick butter
Salt and pepper

Peel and quarter potatoes and place in a three quart pan with water. Boil until they are pierced easily with a fork. Drain. Use a potato ricer and rice the potatoes and roasted garlic cloves back into the hot pan. Microwave the butter and sour cream until melted. Add hot butter mixture with salt and pepper. Whip briefly. If too stiff, add a bit of warm chicken broth until you achieve desired consistency.

*Take head of garlic and cut off the top exposing the bottom 2/3 of the head. Rub head with olive oil. Wrap head in foil in place in oven at 375 for 25 minutes. Remove and allow to cool. When cool, remove foil and squeeze each clove carefully to extract the sweet roasted garlic.

Nubi di Cielo

This dish was invented here at Casa Cebadillas. It happened by chance when we actually found Mostachones in the village. We needed a dessert for this meal and made this and it was a hit.

Lady fingers, pound cake or mostachones
Rum/amaretto
Crème fraiche
Turron, nougat or dulce de leche ice-cream (even vanilla is fine)
6 chocolate truffles

QUICK TIP *This can be made several days even weeks in advance!*

PREPARATION:
Line a metal bread loaf pan with plastic wrap to where it overhangs on the sides. Set I quart of ice-cream on the counter until it begins to soften slightly. Mix the ice-cream with the remainder of the crème fraiche from the amuse course.

Place six chocolate truffles in the microwave until soft and liquid. Set aside.

ASSEMBLY
Place on the bottom of the pan a layer of mostachones or your chosen alternative. Sprinkle this layer with a few tablespoons of amaretto or rum. Now, drizzle a teaspoon of chocolate. Now take one half of the ice-cream and spread over this mixture and smoothing out to the sides. Add another layer of mostachones, drizzle with liquor again, chocolate and the second half of the ice cream. Drizzle remaining chocolate and a final layer of mostachones and drizzle with liquor. Place a small piece of wax paper over this layer and then fold the overhanging plastic wrap over the top and place in the freezer over-night.

To serve: Remove from freezer and unwrap top plastic and remove wax paper. With the plastic wrap overhanging on the sides, carefully pull the dessert out of the bread loaf pan onto and turn over onto a serving platter, carefully peel away the plastic wrap. Serve in thick slices and garnish with fresh whipped cream.

QUICK TIP A really easy dessert for this theme can be made the day before. Allow one quart of vanilla ice cream to soften. Stir in one cup of sour cream and one cup glacéed fruits. Return ice-cream to freezer for at least 8 hours.

NOTE – There really is no good substitute for real whipped cream. In truth, there are whipped toppings that are made from petroleum and actually make a nice floor wax but not a good dessert topping. If you do not want to consume cream you can use alternatives such as a fruit sauce by blending fresh fruit with sugar in a blender, or just use fresh fruit or even a sprig of mint. At Casa Cebadillas we use a traditional whipped cream canister with charger. You add fresh cream, vanilla and sugar, close the top, shake, then add a CO2 charge and you have whipped cream on demand. You can find these products on our on-line store to be delivered to your home on www.spain-vacation-holiday.com, select the tab "Tienda/Store."

South East Asian Experience

Singapore Sling Cocktail

Famous Raffles Hotel cocktail created at the turn-of-the-century

Chinese Tea Smoked Duck

Chilled Tea Smoked Duck Breast with a Guava Lime Glaze and Indonesian Pickled Cucumber garnish

PHỞ

Vietnamese Meatball Soup in a star anise scented broth

Fresh Spring Roll

Spring Rolls with Vietnamese and Thai Dipping Sauces

Thai Green Chicken Curry

Curry made with coriander, lime leaves and spices

Thai Red Beef Curry

Red chilies and lemongrass are made subtle with coconut milk

Jasmine Rice

Steamed aromatic rice

Home-made Ginger Ice-Cream

Vanilla custard with candied ginger ice-cream

If you have a busy schedule, this is the menu for you. The entire dinner can be made the day before with many items made two to three days before and assembled and heated the day of the event. Décor is simple with clean lines. One single flower standing tall as a center piece, have chop sticks and bamboo. Background music from Thailand and Indonesia, perhaps a water feature and lots of candles will give a zen like quality to your dinner experience.

Singapore Sling

I love this cocktail. It goes down too easily! I remember being at Raffles in Singapore with my parents. We were shelling peanuts and sipping our Singapore Slings. We all thought maybe the drinks were watered down because we each drank two rather quickly. We all agreed that they were weak drinks and so my father ordered another round, however he said, "We would like a 'nutter' Wing-a-pore Sing". After we all stopped laughing hysterically we suddenly had the realization, these drinks are potent and that it would be difficult to stand without holding on to something steady!

2 oz. gin
1 oz. cherry brandy
2 oz. sweet-n-sour (see recipe on page 141)
Carbonated Water

In a tall sling or tubo glass, fill with ice and add the gin, cherry brandy and sweet-n-sour, top with carbonated water. Garnish with a lime wedge.

> *NOTE – There are many versions of this famous cocktail that vary from the original. We used ingredients that were available to us. Please use the very simple sweet-n-sour recipe in the back of the book and never buy commercial sweet-n-sour mix, I can't stress this enough, it has made a huge difference in taste for all the cocktails we serve.*

Tea Smoked Duck

To marinate duck – *This appetizer is begun 2 days prior to your dinner*
1 large (3/4 to 1 pound) boneless Moulard* duck breast half with skin
1/8 teaspoon freshly ground black pepper
2 1/8 teaspoon fine sea salt
2 scallions, white and light green parts only, finely chopped
1/4 teaspoon ground cinnamon
1/8 teaspoon ground ginger
1 whole star anise crushed to release the flavor

Rinse breast thoroughly and pat dry. Using a sharp knife, score skin in ¼ inch cross thatch, do not cut through fat into meat below. Sprinkle with 1/8 tsp salt and the pepper.

In large bowl, stir together scallions, cinnamon, ginger, 1/8 tsp salt and the crushed star anise. Add duck breast and roll through the mixture making sure it is completely covered with the mixture. Cover and chill for a minimum of 8 hours, for best results let marinade overnight.

To smoke duck — *This step takes place one day before your dinner*

1 teaspoon Darjeeling tea leaves
1 tablespoon fresh cilantro leaves, coarsely chopped
¼ cup dry rice

You can use a Wok, an electric Wok or we use a small portable outdoor smoker. Line the bottom of your smoker or wok with heavy foil and also the inside of the lid leaving approximately a 3 inch overhang along edges.

In a small bowl stir together the tea leaves, cilantro and the rice. Sprinkle the mixture in an even layer on the bottom of your smoker or wok and place the rack inside, the rack should rest about 2 inches from the bottom.

Next, heat a heavy skillet over medium high heat until hot, but not smoking. Remove duck breast from marinade and place skin side down in skillet. Sear without moving until skin is deep golden brown, approximately 5 minutes.

Using tongs, transfer breast, skin side up to the rack in the wok. Heat Wok on high heat uncovered until steady wisps of smoke begin to appear. Reduce heat to moderate, cover with lid and with oven mitts, fold foil overhang from wok an lid together, crimping to seal tightly (foil will be very hot). Smoke the duck for 10 minutes. Remove from wok, allow to cool, place in container and refrigerate.

Sauce

1 cups Guava Nectar
½ cup Orange Juice
¼ cup Red Wine Vinegar
¼ cup Fresh Lime Juice to taste

Place all ingredients in a saucepan and stir to blend, simmer on low until the mixture begins to thicken. Cool, place in container and refrigerate. Remember the sauce will continue to thicken as it is chilled. If sauce is too thick when it is time to serve, place container in microwave for 2 to 3 seconds just until it is to the consistency for drizzling.

Indonesian Pickled Cucumber – *This garnish is prepared a minimum of 2 days before the dinner and can be made up to a week in advance depending on the level of pickling you desire.*

½ Onion
1 Chili Pepper
¾ cup white vinegar
¼ cup water
3 – 4 TB Sugar
1 tsp Salt
3 Peppercorns
1 Cucumber – sliced into ¼ inch rounds
2-3 whole cloves

Place onion, chili, sugar, salt and peppercorns in a medium sized saucepan and bring to a boil over medium-high heat. Stir in the sliced cucumber, cover tightly and remove from heat. Let rest for 30 to 45 minutes.

Transfer the contents of the saucepan to a storage container and refrigerate.

QUICK TIP: this starter is begun 48 hours before the event making this dinner ideal when hosting solo.

Vietnamese Noodle Soup – *This is prepared the day before*

10 cups Beef Broth
2 medium Onions
4 ½ inch thick slices fresh Ginger
2 TB Fish Sauce
3 Large Garlic Cloves
2 Star Anise broken to release the flavor
1 ½ tsp whole Cloves
Vermicelli

Combine first 7 ingredients in a large soup pot and bring to a boil, reduce heat to low and let simmer 30 to 45 minutes. Strain broth into a large bowl using a sieve, discard the solids. Allow to cool completely, refrigerate.

For noodles, bring a large pot of water to boil, remove from heat. Add noodles to the pot and let stand until tender (approximately 15 minutes). Drain and using kitchen shears cut the noodles into 2-inch lengths. Transfer to a bowl, cover and refrigerate.

Meatballs — *This is prepared the day before*

1 small White Onion
2 cloves Garlic
1 lb. Veal mince
1 TB Kecap Manis
1 TB Soy Sauce

To make meatballs combine all ingredients and form into teaspoon size rounded balls, place on a tray. Heat a 12-inch skillet, place meatballs in skillet and brown on each side. Allow to cool, place in container and refrigerate.

Garnish

Bean Sprouts
Thai Basil (purple)
Lime wedges
Hot Pepper Sliced
Sambal Oolek

The day of the dinner, place the soup in a pot on low heat two hours before your start time. The aroma of this flavorful soup will greet your guests and the help set the tone for the evening. Allow the noodles to come to room temperature before using. Prepare your garnish. When ready to serve this course, reheat the meatballs in microwave. In the bottom of individual serving bowls, place a handful of noodles and 3 to 5 meatballs depending on the size bowl you are using. Ladle the steaming hot soup over the noodles and meatballs. Serve with individual garnishments or place the garnishments on large plates in the center of the table and allow your guests to flavor their soup as they wish.

QUICK TIP: this item is made in advance. We use Sambal Oolek as that was our availability; however the traditional spicy garnish is Sra Cha, easily found in most Asian sections of supermarkets.

Chilled Vegetable Spring Rolls

Spring Roll Wrappers
Lettuce Leaves
Tofu
Prawns
Basil
Mint
Cilantro
Cucumber
Bean Sprouts
Vietnamese Vermicelli

Prior to assembling the spring rolls all ingredients must be dry.

Clean lettuce leaves and pat dry, if using home grown basil, mint and cilantro do the same. Most commercially grown herbs have been cleaned prior to packaging as any moisture causes them to mildew in the package. Peel the cucumber and slice it and the tofu into rectangular pieces approximately three inches long.

If using fresh prawns; clean, peel, devein and drop into boiling water scented with lemon for 30 to 45 seconds, do not overcook as they will be tough. If using frozen cooked prawns, thaw and pat dry.

Cook the vermicelli and drain, leave covered so they do not dry out.

To make the rolls dip the spring roll wrappers quickly into hot water and leave long enough to make them pliable or not quite al dente, remove them and place on a lint free kitchen cloth and pat them dry. They will continue cooking between the time you remove them from the water and pat them dry. Transfer the wrapper to a cutting board or kitchen work surface that is covered with plastic wrap as the wrapper will not stick to this surface. Place one to two lettuce leaves on a the third of the wrapper that is closest to you leaving approximately 1.5 inches on either side as room for folding. Then place some vermicelli on top of the lettuce and build upward from there (you can use kitchen shears to cut the noodles to the desired length), then place one to two pieces of cucumber, a few bean sprouts, our choice of basil mint or cilantro and either two to three prawns or one to two pieces of tofu. Pull the edge closest to you over the ingredients, fold in the sides toward the center and then roll away from you. The remaining moisture in the wrapper will hold it together.

You can make as many as you want and assemble them in any combination of ingredients. We usually make one per person or two per person if only the small wrappers are available. To serve cut diagonally into two pieces and stand them on end or lay them flat turned outward so your guests can see the burst of colors on the inside. We like to serve with two sauces as we've found that most people like to try the taste combination that both sauces provide.

Sauce 1 —

½ cup rice vinegar
½ cup sugar
1 tsp minced garlic
2 TB fish sauce
2 small hot red peppers
1 Tbsp mince carrots

In a small saucepan combine ½ cup water and first three ingredients and bring to a boil, boiling for two minutes over high heat. Remove from heat add the last three ingredients and allow to cool. Transfer sauce to a container and refrigerate.

Sauce 2

1 TB tamarind
2 TB peanut butter
¼ tsp fish sauce
Sambal oolek

Mix the tamarind and creamy peanut butter with the fish sauce and about a teaspoon of sambal oolek (red chili paste). Taste and add more fish sauce or sambal if desired. To make the sauce smoother add drops of water and stir until desired consistency is achieved.

QUICK TIP Both sauces are best made the day before as the flavors blossom. The spring rolls should be made approximately four hours in advance so they have time to chill.

Thai Green Chicken Curry

14 oz. can coconut milk
1 to 4 TB green curry paste (dependent upon your spice tolerance)
1/3 cup vegetable or chicken stock
2 to 3 TB fish sauce
2 TB brown sugar

3 kaffir lime leaves
12 oz. chicken breast cut into 1 inch pieces
1½ cups assorted vegetables cut into 1 inch pieces (red bell pepper, straw mushrooms, carrot or your favorite combination)
½ cup whole Thai basil leaves

In a large sauce pan over medium high heat add the coconut milk, curry paste, stock, fish sauce, brown sugar and lime leaves. Stir thoroughly and allow the sauce to heat to just before boiling, reduce heat to medium low and simmer to thicken slightly. Add the chicken and stir through, then add the vegetables and stir through. Cook until the chicken is done, approximately ten minutes. Just Before serving stir the basil leaves into the mixture and transfer to a serving bowl to be placed on the table and served family style.

Thai Red Beef Curry

14 oz. can coconut milk
1 to 4 TB red curry paste (dependent upon your spice tolerance)
1/3 cup vegetable or chicken stock
2 tsp brown sugar
1 to 2 TB fish sauce
1 cup cherry tomatoes sliced in half
12 oz. sirloin steak sliced into ¼ inch strips
½ cup zucchini
3 stems lemon grass
½ cup snow pea pods

In a large sauce pan over medium high heat add the coconut milk, curry paste, stock, fish sauce and brown sugar. Stir thoroughly and allow the sauce to heat to just before boiling, reduce heat to medium low and simmer to thicken slightly. Add the cherry tomatoes and cook for about five minutes. Then add the strips of beef, zucchini and lemon grass and cook for another five to seven minutes. If your lemon grass has some nice tender ends, slice thinly crosswise and leave in the sauce, the other firm hard pieces are removed and discarded prior to serving. Next add the pea pods and cook an additional minute. Remove from heat and transfer to a serving bowl to be placed on the table and served family style.

QUICK TIP *All ingredients are chopped ahead of time so the actual cook time is less than 20 minutes.*

Jasmine Rice

Prepare rice as package indicates.
A Rice cooker is useful for making this dinner even easier.

Ginger Ice Cream

I cup milk
½ cup sugar
4 egg yolks
I cup cream
1½ tsp vanilla
I inch piece peeled and crushed fresh ginger
¼ cup pulverized crystallized ginger

In a medium saucepan heat the milk and crushed ginger just to the boiling point and remove from heat. Beat sugar and egg yolks together, pour into milk and return to the stove, stirring constantly with a wooden spoon over low heat until the custard coats the back of the spoon. Remove ginger root. Remove from heat and add the pulverized ginger. Cool completely and proceed with your ice-cream maker's manufacture instructions.

QUICK TIP *You can eliminate the fresh and crystallized ginger above and substitute ½ cup ginger jam, adding to the custard before you freeze the ice-cream.*

Photo by Miro Slav
...miro.photo.com for www.casa-cebadillas.com

Photo by Miro Slav OtraVista Photography, España

Una Noche Tranquila

Sangria or Limonada
Selection of Tapas
Gazpacho or Sopa de Ajo Blanco
Potaje
Pollo al Ajillo
Tocino del Cielo
Vino Tinto

This section can be customized to suit your guests tastes. At Casa Cebadillas we provide a large assortment of tapas and a salad or we will have just a few tapas and serve Potaje or Pollo al Ajillo. What is great about Spanish food is that in its simple state is quite elegant and does not need a great deal of preparation. There are so many wonderful recipes with Arabic influence here in Andalucía. These are just a few.

At Casa Cebadillas we enjoy utilizing the colors of the Spanish flag of red and yellow. We usually have a base with a black tablecloth base and then use a red tablecloth turned to expose the black on four corners and use yellow napkins. Plates and service are terracotta and "earthy elegance". Flamenco music in the background during the beginning of the evening and then mellow out the evening with classical Spanish guitar. You can find a selection of Spanish music at our "Tienda" by visiting www.spain-vacation-holiday.com and select "Store / Tienda and download music, purchase CDs or shop for Spanish products to be delivered to your door.

Sangria

I think the most disappointing food item for me in Spain was the commercialization of Sangria. It is difficult to find a true Sangria except at home. Today many restaurants add sugar in a pitcher with pieces of fruit, red wine and lemon-lime soda and tell the tourists it is Sangria. We have even had the experience where they added a can of fruit cocktail. Although "soda" was traditionally used, we use cava. However, in the USA I like adding "Cold Duck" sparking burgundy. You could use other sparkling wines as well. Because the glass has ice, the potency is diluted so we feel club soda is not necessary.

2 bottles red wine
1 bottle sidra, cava or champagne
2 cups seasonal firm fruit cut in slices (save some for garnish)
½ cup juice (orange, apple or pear)
½ cup brandy
¼ cup sugar

The night before you plan to serve, In a large pitcher add brandy and sugar and stir until dissolved. Add one cup of fruit slices and muddle until the fruit is bruised and falling apart slightly. Now add second cup of fruit slices and stir to mix. Add the juice, cover and place in the refrigerator overnight. Place sidra, cava or champagne and the red wine in the refrigerator to chill overnight as well.

Preparation: When ready to serve, pour red wine into pitcher and stir. Now add your sparkling wine and serve immediately in tall glasses with ice.

NOTE — This makes quite a bit of Sangria and you may need to divide into two pitchers.

NON-ALCOHOLIC VERSION: For the designated drivers you can make a sangria with non-alcoholic red wine, fruit and top with sparkling cider.

Limonada

An alternative to Sangria
6 lemons
1 cup sugar
1 bottle dry red wine
1 bottle dry white wine

With a sharp knife or vegetable peeler remove the yellow peel being careful not to get the white pith. Cut the peel into strips about 2 inches long and ½ inch wide. Set them aside. Squeeze juice from one lemon and then slice the remaining 3 unpeeled lemons crosswise into ¼ inch rounds

Combine strips of lemon peel lemon juice lemon slices and sugar into a 4 quart serving pitcher. Pour in red and white wine and stir with a bar spoon until well mixed. Refrigerate for at least 8 hours stirring two or three times.

To serve, stir again taste and add more sugar if you pres the drink sweeter. Serve in chilled wine glasses or tumblers with ice.

Olives

You can marinate your own olives by using the recipe in the Ciao Bella menu or you can simply buy Spanish Olives and serve them. Always taste your olives ahead of time and see if they are too salty. If the brine is strong, rinse the olives or even allow them to soak in water for a few hours, add olive oil and lemon juice and give a toss before serving.

Manchego Cheese Two Ways

A very simple way to serve this cheese is in triangular individual pieces with a slice of membrillo on top (quince paste).

A second way is to serve the triangles but dip a spoon in "miel de caña" and drizzle over the cheese. "Miel de caña" is similar to molasses or treacle.

Manchego cheese is a sheep's milk cheese made in the La Mancha region of Spain. This cheese is aged for three months or longer, and is semi-firm with a rich golden color and small holes. It ranges from mild to sharp, depending on how long it is aged.

NOTE – There are SEVERAL wonderful cheese from Spain you can have on your table for guests to enjoy such as Cabrales, Mahon and Idiazabal. These can just be served plain with an assortment of crackers, bread or biscuits. You can also order these products by going to our website www.spain-vacation-holiday.com and select "tienda/store." Here you will find a complete selection of Spanish food that can be delivered to your front door.

Crusty Rustic Bread

Depending on where you live, you may be able to purchase great rustic bread. If you do not and decide to make your own in a bread machine, remove the dough before baking and roll into a log and allow to raise again. Make slits on top and baste with a raw egg mixed with water to make a hard crust and place in 450 degree oven and then reduce temperature to 375 and bake until brown and hallow when tapped.

Sliced Serrano Ham

Very thin slices of Serrano ham on a plate and guests can add with their cheese or savor the flavor alone.

Gambas pil pil

Shrimp quickly cooked in a garlic chili flavored olive oil.
18 ginormous gambas (ginormous is my definition as the biggest you can find)
Olive Oil
½ tsp pimentón (Spanish paprika)
1 or 2 whole red hot peppers such as cayenne
2 cloves garlic thinly sliced
Pinch salt
Juice of ½ lemon
TB chopped parsley

Clean, peel and devein shrimp (I don't care what you've heard; remove the vein it is NOT sand)! Keep raw shrimp chilled until ready to serve. In a stovetop ovenproof shallow serving dish with sides about 1.5 inches, add olive oil until covers about ¼ inch. Add whole chilies and garlic and put on medium high heat. When garlic starts to bubble and just begins to turn golden, add gambas (shrimp), salt and paprika, stir with a wooden spoon turning Shrimp until they are pink on both sides (this should take about ½ minute depending on the heat of your oil). Squeeze lemon all over and toss parsley on top and serve. The casserole will be hot so make sure to have a hot plate and use pot holders! Serve with lots of crusty bread to dip into the wonderful juices.

Albondigas

Spanish Meatballs

2 lbs. ground meat (equal parts of pork, veal and lamb is best; but pork is traditional)
2 slices bread one inch thick, crusts removed
I whole egg
2 TB parsley
I tsp smoked pimentón (smoked paprika)
I onion chopped
I TB Chinchon seco or other dry anisette
2 cloves garlic minced
Salt and pepper
Olive oil
Flour
½ cup sherry (Jerez) dry or Medium
2 whole bay laurel leaves

Place meat in a large mixing bowl. Process bread in a food processor until it is crumbed and add to meat. Mix meat mixture with egg, parsley, paprika, chopped onion, Chinchon, garlic, salt and pepper until all are thoroughly mixed.

Heat in a frying pan a small amount of olive oil. Roll meat mixture into I inch balls and roll into flour to coat. Place meatballs into hot pan and fry until brown. Remove meatballs and keep warm. Add sherry and deglaze pan scraping up all the brown bits. Add a little more sherry and/or water if the sauce is too thick. Return meatballs and heat until all are thoroughly warm. Serve in a casserole with toothpicks and garnish with parsley.

NOTE — When making your meatballs, do not make them perfectly round as they will not hold the sauce as well and can become dry. We make these in the Spanish cazuelas, earthenware dishes. We use these often as we can to start things on the stove top and put straight into the oven, then onto the table. Saving on washing up!

Gazpacho

Fresh Gazpacho is a wonderfully easy and fresh chilled soup.
It is a great way to get kids to "drink" their salad!
2 medium cucumbers peeled and chopped course
5 medium fresh tomatoes peeled chopped
I large onion
I medium green pepper seeded chopped
2 cloves garlic chopped
4 cups french/italian bread with crust removed
2 cups tomato juice
¼ cup red wine vinegar
4 tsp sea salt
4 TB olive oil
I TB tomato paste
In a blender (at Casa Cebadillas we use a VitaMix which we highly recommend) add all the ingredients and process until liquid. Chill at least 12 hours.

To serve garnish with croutons, chopped onion, chopped green pepper and cucumber. At Casa Cebadillas we serve this with a shot of iced pepper vodka on the side.

Sopa de Ajo Blanco

Chilled garlic soup.

The first time I mentioned this soup to my mother she recoiled over the thought of garlic soup being served cold. When I had her imagine a Vichyssoise with garlic her curiosity was peaked. This soup is very traditional in this area of Spain. It is easy to make and in one word: wonderful!

6 oz. (¾ cup) blanched, peeled almonds
6 slices stale baguette or white bread crusts removed
4 to 5 peeled cloves garlic
6 cups water, COLD
7 TB extra virgin Spanish olive oil
4 to 5 TB Spanish sherry vinegar
Salt to taste

QUICK TIP Use a package of blanched almonds and be delighted you did not have to do this by hand!

Preparation:
If you do not have blanched almonds, you can prepare them by hand. Boil a small pot of water. Add almonds and boil for 2 minutes. Drain and dry on paper towels. The skins will slip off easily.

Peel garlic. Trim crust from bread slices if using French-style or rustic bread. Place bread in one to two cups cold water to soak.

While bread is soaking, place garlic and almonds into a food processor or blender (we recommend a VitaMix to achieve the desired end product). Blend or pulse until smooth. Remove bread from water and squeeze out excess water. Tear bread into quarters and add bread and 1 tsp salt to processor or blender. Blend or pulse on high. While blending, slowly drizzle olive oil, then vinegar, and finally the water into blender or processor. Taste. Adjust salt, vinegar and oil to taste.

Pour into a container or bowl. Seal and chill at least two to three hours or overnight. Serve in chilled bowls or glass mugs, with a splash of vivid green virgin olive oil.

NOTE — Traditionally, this dish is served with a few green grapes as a garnish; we like the contrasting color, however we prefer to substitute olive oil drops.

Pinchitos of Pork

Marinated and grilled pork skewers
2 lbs. cubed pork
Marinade:
¼ cup dry sherry
¼ cup olive oil
1 tsp dry cumin
Fresh cracked pepper (about 4 turns)
3 tsp fresh thyme leaves or ½ tsp dry
2 whole cloves freshly crushed into a few pieces
¼ tpn nutmeg
2 crushed bay leaves
½ tsp red pepper flakes
2 TB minced flat leaf parsley
3 tsp lemon juice
8 cloves garlic peeled and crushed
1 tsp pimentón dulce (sweet Spanish paprika) or smoked
Large pinch of course salt

Make the marinade the day before. Pierce pork with bamboo or metal skewers six to seven inches in length. Place skewers in a sealable food container approximately seven to eight inches in length. Coat each skewer with one tablespoon marinade, cover and place in refrigerator overnight. When you are ready to serve, place on BBQ grill over hot white coals and grill until pork is done. Serve immediately.

Pollo al Ajillo

This is a very simple chicken dish and typical of Spain. Unfortunately, in areas where there are more tourists we are seeing less of this and more "pizza," sigh!
You can prepare this outside on a campfire or BBQ!
6 pieces of chicken with skin
8 TB olive oil
3 whole garlic bulbs (separate cloves but leave skin on)
8 bay leaves
½ cup dry sherry
½ cup dry white wine
¼ cup water
Salt and pepper

In a heavy bottomed frying pan that will accommodate all of the chicken, place olive oil and heat on medium flame. When the oil is hot (test by baptizing with a little water if it spatters it is hot) add garlic cloves and fry until golden. Remove golden cloves and set aside. Add chicken skin side down and fry in oil until golden brown, turn pieces and continue until both sides are golden. Return garlic to pan and add bay leaves and wine and deglaze pan while spooning sauce over chicken and turning chicken in the sauce. Add salt and pepper and shake pan to incorporate the sauce. If you feel there is not enough liquid add the water and cover the pan and reduce to simmer and cook until done (approximately 15 minutes). Taste for seasoning before serving.

Salad Arturo

6 plum tomatoes in wedges
1 large cucumber sliced crosswise
3 green onions chopped
1 small green bell pepper in one inch pieces
24 black Spanish olives or other brine cured olives
8 oz (250 grams) cubed goat cheese
2 very small hearts of romaine chopped
Salt and pepper to taste
¼ cup Extra Virgin Olive Oil
2 Tablespoons Fresh squeezed Lemon Juice

Place the olive oil, lemon juice, garlic, salt and pepper in a small jar with a screw-top lid and shake to combine. Place all the salad ingredients in a large bowl. Pour the dressing over the salad and toss gently to combine just before serving.

Potaje de Garbanzos

Marriage of Moorish and Roman Cuisine in Andalucia

I will never forget the first time I had Potaje here in Andalucía. I was on a coach trip to Doñana National Park and the hotel was offering a thick hearty soup as a first course. I passed on the main course and requested another bowl of this wonderful Potaje. They were so excited that an extranjero (foreigner) thought this dish was "estar de muerte" (to die for) they gave me the recipe.

This dish is perfect to serve with just a salad and crusty bread. Enjoy!

1 1/3 lbs chickpeas, dried
5½ cups water
8 garlic cloves peeled
3 bay leaves
1/3 lb. salt pork/slab bacon
1 ham bone
3 TB olive oil (Spanish for authenticity)
3 slices bread, ½ inch thick (crusty or rustic style)
1/3 cup Spanish ham (bit sized pieces)
1 large onion finely chopped
3 Spanish chorizos sliced thick
1 tsp paprika
1 lb. Swiss chard or collard greens, coarsely chopped
1 lb. small red potatoes, peeled (about 2 inches in diameter or larger potatoes cut in 2 inch chunks)
Salt to taste
16 blanched almonds, finely chopped
3 hard-boiled eggs

Directions
Soak the chickpeas overnight in a large pot of cold water to cover, drain.

In the large pot combine chickpeas, 4 cups water, garlic, bay leaves, slab bacon, and bone; bring to a boil, cover and simmer about 1½ hours.

Meanwhile, in a medium skillet heat the oil and sauté the bread slices until golden on both sides. Remove and reserve the bread.

Add the ham and onion to the skillet, sauté until the onion has wilted. Stir in the paprika and remove the pan from the heat.

Add the onion mixture to the chickpeas and stir. Add the greens, potatoes, and salt to taste to the chickpeas and continue cooking 30 minutes or more, or until the chickpeas and potatoes are tender. Remove the ham bone.

In a mortar or food processor, combine the sautéed bread, almonds, four tablespoons of the chickpeas from the pot, and the yolks of the hard-boiled eggs; mash to a paste. Stir the paste into the stew, cover and let sit 10 minutes before serving.

Chop the hard-boiled egg whites.

Divide the potaje into soup bowls and garnish with chopped hard-boiled egg whites.

Tocino del cielo

This was originally a dessert we served instead of flan. This recipe has the addition of cake which is not traditional, just something we did to make it a little more unique.
1 cup sweetened condensed milk (200 ml can)
6 eggs (4 yolks 2 whole)
1 cup skim milk (for creamy texture)
¼ cup sugar

Make a caramel sauce by adding one cup sugar into a heavy sauce pan over medium heat. Do not stir but tilt the pan and cook watching carefully. After about five minutes when it is dark golden brown, take a heavy spoon and stir, prepare to work quickly (*CAUTION, hot sugar burns are horrible… trust me I know!*). Pour this caramel in the cake pan and tilt to coat all the sides. Work quickly because it will harden fast.

Mix four egg yolks and two whole eggs until blended. Stir sweetened condensed milk and skim milk into the mixture and continue until all is well mixed. Pour contents into cake pan.

For the optional cake:
3 egg yolks
¼ cup sugar
¾ cup cake flour
½ tsp of baking powder

¼ cup of skim milk
3 egg whites
¼ cup sugar

Beat three egg yolks until creamy with ¼ cup sugar. Add flour and baking powder and beat until a thick batter is formed. Slowly add skim milk and mix batter thoroughly. Beat egg whites with sugar until stiff peaks are formed. Take a large spoonful of beaten egg whites and fold into batter. Now add remaining beaten egg whites and fold carefully to keep the air and volume. With a rubber spatula pour into cake pan.

Place the cake pan in a larger pan half-filled with hot (not boiling) water (Bain Marie). Bake in a preheated 350°F oven for 50 minutes to an hour. After 50 minutes, insert a toothpick at the center of the cake. If it comes out clean, the cake is done. If not, bake a few minutes longer, testing every five minutes or so.

To serve:
This cake should be served at room temperature. Unmold the dessert in the following fashion: run a butter knife around the edges, you should see bits of caramel sauce appear. This is a good thing! Now get your serving plate and place on top of the cake pan and quickly invert. Stop for a second and breathe. Now slowly lift the cake pan and when you see the caramel sauce dripping down into the fluffy cake, privately jump around in the kitchen doing a victory dance exclaiming "YES… I did it I did it!" then compose yourself and present to your guests as if this is something you do daily.

A Big Fat Greek Dinner

Cucumber Cooler
Cocktail made with cucumber and thyme

Hummus with Roasted Red Peppers
Garbanzo bean puree with garlic and tahini served with flat bread and a roasted red pepper salad

Dolmathes
Grape Leaves stuffeed with rice and currants and pine nuts

Saganaki
Searing hot pan with a hard cheese flamed with Ouzo and served with bread... OPA!

Ensalada Greek Style
Greek Salad with Kalamata olives, onions, tomatoes, feta cheese with a garlic lemon dressing

Pastitsio
Ziti casserole with mince, tomato, garlic and topped with a Béchamel sauce

Roast Lamb with Rosemary, Lemon and Garlic
Leg of Lamb roasted in a wood fired brick oven

Spanakopita
Spinach and feta in a filo crust

Tzatziki
Greek yogurt and garlic sauce

Fresh Figs stuffed with cheese and orange

I love Greek cuisine and the how the Greeks love their food and celebration of life. This menu makes a tremendous amount of food and should be savored for hours serving course after course between wines and perhaps shots of Ouzo.

At Casa Cebadillas, we have a traditional wood fired brick oven which gives lamb a wonderful earthy, smoky flavor which blends perfectly with Tzatziki. If you do not have a wood fired brick oven you can sear the lamb in a very hot oven preheated at 500 degrees. After the lamb has seared for fifteen minutes, turn down to 350 without opening the oven door. This will sear the fat quickly and give you a wonderful crust. OPA!

Cucumber Cooler

6 two inch pieces of peeled cucumber
3 tsp fresh thyme (½ tsp dry)
4 oz. simple syrup
12 oz. vodka

Place cucumber, thyme and simple syrup in the blender and blend on high until liquid. Pour into a large pitcher. Add vodka, stir and chill. When ready to serve you can either, stir and pour over ice or at Casa Cebadillas we put the cocktail in the VitaMix and add ice and create a slush type drink that is very refreshing on a hot summer day.

NOTE – Do not add vodka in the blender with cucumber. The result will be a very foamy drink. Besides, it bruises the liquor!

Hummus with Roasted Red Peppers with Pita *

*See recipes under Moroccan Influences page 29

Dolmathes

I medium onion finely chopped
¼ cup olive Oil
I cup rice
¼ cup parsley
¼ cup currants
I TB fresh dill or I tsp dry
I TB fresh mint or ½ teaspoon dry
2 lemons, juiced
2 TB pine nuts
I jar grape leaves or I pkg soaked in fresh water.
Lemon wedges

Cook rice as instructed until "al dente" and set aside off heat when done. Sauté pine nuts in olive oil, when they are just starting to turn golden, add onions and sauté until soft but not brown. Add rice and stir to mix and lightly. Cook rice according to directions with half the lemon juice as the liquid.

Add dill, mint, parsley and currants. Rinse grape leaves in cold water, remove stems and place one tablespoon of rice mixture on dull side folding in the sides and rolling up leaves. Put in a 10x13 inch pan, open end down. Cover with ¼ cup olive oil and juice of a lemon and enough water to cover at least 1/2 the dolmathes. Cover with any remaining grape leaves, or the ones that were too small to use, cover with aluminum foil and place in a 375° oven for 45 minutes. You can also cook on the stove top on low for 45 minutes. When cool, remove the aluminum foil and do the victory dance in the kitchen. Cover with plastic wrap and chill for at least one day. When ready to serve place on serving tray, garnish with lemon slices and tzatziki.

> NOTE – Use a very small amount of salt in the rice if your grape leaves are brined otherwise you will end up with an overly salted result.

> QUICK TIP This in one of the rare times I will use canned or tinned products. An old Greek friend of mine (well she was not old but she is not my friend anymore) told me that the canned ones were not too bad if you serve them very chilled and add a high quality olive oil on top and a squeeze of lemon right before serving. That was one of the few things she was right about… they are not bad, and do save a great deal of time.

Saganaki

At Casa Cebadillas we had some difficulty with this particular dish. It is imperative that this dish is served hot in order to be flamed at the table. We had 21 stairs from the kitchen to the terrace where the dinners are served. By the time we would reach the serving table we would get nothing but a little sputter of a flame. One day, I decided to try adding a little absinthe to the Ouzo. Running as fast as we could to the serving table we poured the ouzo with absinthe and ignited it. There was a bursting explosion and the flame singed my eyebrows and we could not stop laughing as we exclaimed OPA! We have found that different brands of Ouzo create a different sized flame. Practice using a hot pan, take it off the heat for a moment and add your liquor and ignite (mind your eyebrows) and adjust your liquor to get a nice flare-up. If Absinthe is not available you can add a small amount of 100 proof vodka to increase the flame.

The cheese used is usually Kefalograviera, Kasseri, Kefalotyri, or sheep's milk Feta cheese. The name Saganaki comes from the pan in which it is made. A sagani is a two-handled pan that is made in many different materials. In the market, look for a small paella pan, small cast iron skillet, or even an oval au gratin dish in a pinch.

The key to success with this dish is to get the oil hot (just before it starts to smoke) before frying.

8 oz. kefalotyri, kasseri or firm feta cheese
½ cup of olive oil
I beaten egg
I/3 cup of flour
I/3 cup corn starch
Fresh ground pepper
I lemon cut in half and tied in cheese cloth
¼ cup Ouzo Absinthe combination.

Take the slice of cheese and soak it in cold water for six hours. When ready to serve, remove from water and place in a dish with the beaten egg and turn to coat. In a separate dish, mix flour, corn starch and a few grinds of fresh pepper. Moisten each side in the egg and dredge in the flour cornstarch.

In a small heavy-bottomed frying pan (cast-iron works best), heat the olive oil over medium-high heat until very hot but not smoking, place the cheese in the pan and sear each side until golden-brown on both sides. Meanwhile have a sagani or small heavy paella pan heated ready to present to the table.

When ready to serve, first be sure you have a hot pad at the table. Also be sure YOU have a pot holder to protect yourself. Have a lighter, lemon half and Ouzo at the table. Place the fried cheese into the hot sagani pan and briskly bring to the table, add the Ouzo ignite and exclaim,

OPA! Now take the lemon and squeeze over the flame to extinguish. Return utensils to the kitchen and when you are quite sure no one is looking do the Victory Dance!

Ensalada Greek Style

Greek Salad with Kalamata olives, onions, tomatoes, feta cheese with a garlic lemon dressing.

A *good* Greek salad, is a rough country salad of juicy plum tomatoes, crisp cucumber, sliced red onion, green pepper, crumbly feta cheese and kalamata olives. Serve this delightful combination as a side dish with some crusty bread.

¼ cup Extra Virgin Olive Oil
2 Tablespoons Fresh squeezed Lemon Juice
1 clove garlic finely minced
1 teaspoon dried oregano (2 teaspoons fresh)
¼ teaspoon sea salt
¼ teaspoon freshly ground black pepper
8 oz (250 grams) cubed feta cheese
24 Kalamata olives

Place the olive oil, lemon juice, garlic, salt, pepper and oregano in a small jar with a screw-top lid and shake to combine. Place all the salad ingredients in a large bowl. Pour the dressing over the salad and toss gently to combine just before serving. Garnish the Greek salad with a little freshly ground black pepper.

Pastitsio

Prepare meat sauce:
1 lb. ground lamb
1 onion chopped
1 garlic clove finely chopped
3 TB olive oil
1 cup red wine
1 6 oz. can tomato paste
½ cup strong beef stock
2 TB parsley
Salt and Pepper

Brown lamb in olive oil and when almost cooked through, add onions and garlic and sauté until lamb is cooked. Deglaze pan with red wine and add remaining ingredients except tomato paste. Cook on low for one hour. Add tomato paste, return to heat and simmer for 15 minutes. If the sauce becomes too thick add a touch more beef stock. The sauce should be thick.

Prepare Ziti:
16 oz. pkg Ziti type pasta
5 TB butter
½ cup fresh parmesan cheese grated
¼ tsp nutmeg
3 eggs beaten
Salt and pepper

Bring to boil a large pot of salted water. Add Ziti and cook until al dente. Drain and return to the pot, add butter and toss to coat. Add ¼ cup cheese and nutmeg and toss again. Allow to cool, then add the eggs, salt and pepper and stir again.

Prepare béchamel:
1/3 cup butter
½ cup flour
3 cups milk
¼ tsp nutmeg
Salt and pepper to taste
1 egg beaten

Melt butter, add flour and cook roux stirring constantly until smooth but not brown. Add milk and stir constantly with a wire whisk and bring to a boil. Add nutmeg and salt and pepper. Taste and correct seasonings. Let the sauce cool, then stir in the beaten egg.

Assembly:
Take a buttered au gratin dish or 13 x 9 x 3 inch casserole and butter the bottom and sides. Spoon ½ the Ziti mix evenly on the bottom, then top with the meat sauce. Cover this layer with the second half of the ziti mixture. Now pour the béchamel sauce over the top and sprinkle the remaining ¼ cup parmesan cheese and bake in a 350 degree oven for 45 to 50 minutes.

Roast Lamb with Rosemary and Lemon

This dish we prepare in our wood fired brick oven. If you have one… GREAT! But, we are assuming most people do not. This recipe is to create a similar product in your kitchen.

Lamb legs in Spain are very small. For a party of 6 we use two lamb legs. In the USA lamb legs are quite large. Ask your butcher for the smallest leg possible approximately four to five pounds.

1 leg of lamb
2 heads of garlic, cloves peeled
4 lemons
Olive oil
BIG handful of Fresh Rosemary with stems
12 small red potatoes or 6 medium brown peeled potatoes
2 Carrots cut in thick 2 inch sections
Kosher salt
Pepper grinds
½ cup white wine

The day before, wash and dry your lamb leg. Salt the outside. Make slits all along the leg and insert peeled cloves of garlic. Use at least one entire head of garlic. Place the lamb in a large plastic bag, add ½ cup olive oil and squeeze three lemons in and toss the rinds in the bag as well. Place in the refrigerator and turn a couple times until the next day.

Preheat oven to the highest temperature 450 to 500 degrees.

The size of your lamb will dictate the length of cooking time. You have two choices; either cook the lamb and hold it until serving or cook the lamb and pray it is ready when the guests are.

About an hour before you would like to serve the lamb, remove from the refrigerator and let sit at room temperature for at least 15 minutes. Place ½ the rosemary stems on the bottom of the pan. Remove the leaves from the second half of the rosemary stems and set aside, place these naked stems on the bottom of the pan along with the others. Place marinated leg of lamb on top of the rosemary. Sprinkle salt and pepper on the lamb. Add remaining marinade into the pan along with the potatoes and carrots. Add white wine to the pan and add the second garlic head of peeled cloves. Place lamb in the middle of the oven.

Cook lamb for 30 minutes without opening the oven. If you have a window in your oven door, peek to see that the lamb should be getting very brown. Once it begins to get VERY brown, open the oven (*watch for steam*), stir vegetable and baste lamb. Close the door and reduce heat to 350. At this point you should monitor for doneness. When you pierce the lamb, the juices should be rosy. Once this has been achieved, remove from oven and tent with foil and wait at least 10 to 15 minutes before carving. If the guests are not ready, you can return the lamb to a warm oven, tented until ready to serve.

> *NOTE – Always let your lamb rest before serving. The first time we prepared this lamb was in our wood fired brick oven. The day of the dinner, the host phoned us to say they changed their mind and wanted us to prepare dinner in their house. We agreed and went to inspect the house. There was one thing missing in this house which was a traditional Andalucian home AN OVEN! I explained to the host I cannot cook a lamb at one end of town and prepare her dinner at the other end of the village! What we ended up doing was once the lamb was cooked in the wood burning oven, the entire pan with the lamb was wrapped in several layers of foil, then several layers of beach blankets and then placed in a wheeled duffle bag and wheeled across the cobblestoned streets to the host's home. When it was served, it was still warm and I have to say it was the juiciest most succulent lamb we have ever prepared! The reason for this, the lamb had sufficient time to reabsorb juices before it was served.*

Tzatziki

Begin this sauce the day before and finish making it about three hours before you serve to allow the flavors to meld.
16 oz. plain yogurt
1 garlic clove minced
1 cucumber
1 TB fresh mint leaves chopped

Place yogurt in a sieve and allow to drain 12 to 24 hours. If the holes in your sieve are too course line the sieve with cheese cloth. When ready transfer yogurt to a small mixing bowl, the yogurt should be very thick after the water all the water has drained and yield about 1½ cups. Add the garlic and stir to combine. Slice one end off the cucumber and peel about half down. Using the tines of a fork, scrape the cucumber over the bowl allowing the juice to fall into the yogurt, scrape until the flesh is soft and bruised and then with your hand squeeze the cucumber to juice it into the yogurt being careful not to let any seeds drop in. When the cucumber is dry, stir the juice through the yogurt and add the fresh mint. Taste and adjust with more cucumber or mint. I always use only one clove of garlic because the garlic flavor will blossom by serving time. You can also seed and very finely chop the remaining flesh until resembles minced garlic and add to the yogurt to enhance the cool cucumber flavor by serving time.

Spanakopita

We have had guests tell us they do not like spinach, never have liked it and never will like it. They begrudgingly try a piece of this and their eyes widen and they exclaim "My WORD, this spinach pie is absolutely BRILL".

Olive oil
2 bunches green onion (spring onion) with green tops
1 TB fresh parsley
1 tsp dill
3 ten oz. bags frozen chopped spinach
8 oz. cream cheese
8 oz. feta cheese crumbled
8 oz. cottage cheese
3 TB parmesan cheese
5 eggs well beaten
1 box phyllo pastry thawed
1 stick butter

Saute onion in a small amount of olive oil until soft. Add parsley and dill and set aside.

Microwave the spinach until completely defrosted. Place spinach in a clean tea towel and twist as hard as you can to squeeze out as much water as possible.

In a mixing bowl, add drained spinach, cream cheese, parmesan cheese, cottage cheese, crumbled feta and onion mixture. Stir to blend. Add the beaten eggs and stir the filling until incorporated.

Melt butter. Using a pastry brush butter a 9 x 13 x 3 inch baking dish. Line the bottom half of the dish with ½ the phyllo buttering between each layer. Add the spinach filling and smooth the top. Place the remaining phyllo on top buttering each layer. Once assembled, precut the serving slices before baking, cutting only down through the top layer. Bake at 350 until brown and crispy on top 45 minutes to 1 hour.

> **QUICK TIP** *You can make the filling the day before you prepare the pie or you can make the entire pie and freeze it and cook another day.*

Figs stuffed with cheese and orange

After this large meal you really don't need much of a dessert. We serve a simple dessert and we top with one of two toppings. You can decide which one you prefer.

18 fresh figs (we prefer the black variety, but the green work well also)
Brie cheese
Mandarin orange slices, drained

Cut off the stem of fig, but the leaving a tip; make a slice from the top of the fig about half way down. Stuff each fig with a slice of brie and an orange section. Lay three figs on each plate and drizzle whichever topping you select.

Topping 1:
¼ cup balsamic vinegar
1 TB sugar
In a small cook balsamic and sugar until a thick syrup is achieved and drizzle on dates.
Topping 2:
¼ cup chopped toasted walnuts
3 TB honey
½ tsp miel de caña or molasses
Dash of cinnamon
Tiny pinch clove
Mix together and drizzle over dates

Vegetarian Moussaka

Eggplant
1 small onion chopped
3 garlic cloves
½ cup red wine
1 tsp marmite
24 oz. can whole tomatoes
6 oz. can tomato paste
¼ tsp cinnamon
2 large eggplant
Béchamel sauce (see pastitsio)
½ cup parmesan cheese

Make a tomato sauce by sautéing three cloves garlic and onion in olive oil. Add tomatoes, red wine and marmite. Simmer for I hour. Add tomato paste until desire consistency is achieved. Add ¼ teaspoon cinnamon to the sauce.

Peel eggplant and slice into rounds about ½ inch thick. Salt each side and set aside for an hour to drain. Wipe with a paper towel and place in a baking pan, brush with olive oil and place under the broiler until lightly brown. Turn slices over and repeat.

Assembly:
Grease a 13 x 9 x 3 inch baking dish. Add a little of the tomato sauce and spread across to cover the bottom of the dish. Add a layer of eggplant and a little of the cheese. Add another layer of tomato sauce and cheese. Add another layer of eggplant, cheese and remainder or sauce. Top layer should be eggplant only. Now add béchamel a little parmesan and bake for one hour at 350 degrees.

Photo by Miro Slav
www.mirophoto.com for www.casa-cebadillas.com

Photo by Miro Slav OtraVista Photography, España

An Evening in Provence

Champagne Moisson de Mason
Champagne cocktail with seasonal fruit

Fromage de chèvre et Tapenade
Goat Cheese and homemade tapenade

Salade (vert) Sauvage
Wild Baby Green Salad

Boeuf Bourguignon
Classic French Dish of Beef Braised in Red Wine

Purée de Pommes de Terre
Mashed potatoes with cream and butter

Petit Pois de Campagne
Peas prepared country style

Crêpes Noisette au Chocolat
Crepes filled with pureed hazelnuts and chocolate

A country French dinner is versatile and subtly elegant. The menu items are from typical meals my mother prepared growing up. To this day, Boeuf Bourguignon is my comfort food. What is great about this theme is that it allows you more time with your guests. Boeuf Bourguignon is never at its best the day it is prepared, but rather the following day! For music I love playing classical cello selections. The dinner above is a wonderful compliment to a hearty red wine and rustic bread.

An Evening in Provence Recipes:

Champagne Moisson de Mason

Fresh Fruit either Pear*, Cherries or Apple** or peaches***
White wine (enough to cover)
Champagne
¼ cup portwine
¼ cup sugar
¼ cup brandy

Take selected fruit and place in a sauce pan where they are not crowded but can move.

Add sugar and white wine to cover. Bring to a boil and reduce heat. Continue cooking fruit until just beginning to become soft. Remove from liquid and set aside. Boil down wine and sugar until it becomes thick. Add port wine and continue to boil for 1 minute. Remove from heat and return fruit and allow to cool. Add brandy and chill fruit overnight.

To serve, place one piece of fruit in each flute. Add equal portions of brandy poaching liquid (approximately 2 tablespoons) in each flute. Top with chilled champagne and serve.

*if using tiny pears, select 3 so each half can go in a flute. Peel before poaching.
**if using apples I cored tart apple cut into 6 chunks
***if using tiny peaches, blanche first to remove skin

Fromage de chèvre et Tapenade

8 oz. log goat cheese
3 garlic cloves
6 oz. can of drained anchovies (omit for vegetarians)
12 oz. can of black olives pitted
1 shake of salsa picante like Tabasco®
1 tsp capers
2 TB extra virgin olive oil
Rustic crackers (whole grain)

Using a hand-held blender mix in a tall narrow container or in a small food processor, add garlic and anchovies. Pulse until they become a paste. Add olives, picante sauce and pulse again. Add capers and pulse until it has the appearance of caviar. If too thick you can add olive oil until desired consistency is achieved but be careful not to make it runny. It should be very thick.

To serve:
Spoon the tapenade into a shallow serving dish. Place a very small dollop of sour cream (about ½ teaspoon) and a small sprig of fresh dill for garnish. Serve the tapenade along side the goat cheese and rustic crackers. Guests can spread goat cheese on a cracker and add tapenade on top or enjoy either alone.

> *QUICK TIP This can be made up to two days in advance and kept in the refrigerator.*

Salade (vert) Sauvage

2 bags cleaned wild greens
Fresh vine-ripe fruit or produce du jour such as apples and pears
Raisins, grapes, pine nuts and dried cherries or cranberries for garnish
Raspberry Maple Vinaigrette:
¼ cup raspberry vinegar*
¼ cup olive oil
¼ cup vegetable oil
¼ cup pure maple syrup
I TB dijon mustard
I TB dried tarragon leaves, crushed
Dash salt or pepper to taste

Place all the vinaigrette ingredients into a cruet and shake or you can blend with a blender.

Assembly:
Place greens in a salad bowl and add 3 tablespoons vinaigrette and toss to coat. Place serving on each plate and add cut slices of fruit du jour and sprinkle each with a little more dressing. Garnish plates with raisins, grapes, pine nuts, dried cherries or cranberries.

* If you don't have raspberry vinegar you can use ¼ cup red wine vinegar along with I teaspoon raspberry jam and blend together.

Alternative dressing:
Olive oil, fresh lemon juice, salt and pepper.

Boeuf Bourguignon for 12

This recipe is for twelve instead of six. The reason is so you can store half in the freezer and serve at a later time.

6 lbs. chuck beef cut in large cubes
Flour, salt and pepper to dredge
¼ cup butter and ¼ cup olive oil and sauté beef Add
¼ cup warm cognac
½ lb. salt pork lardons
4 garlic cloves chopped
2 carrots sliced
2 leeks sliced
4 medium onions chopped
2 TB fresh parsley chopped
2 bay leaves
2 tsp thyme (1 tsp dry)
1 bottle burgundy or red table wine

In a large mixing bowl add beef cubes, flour, salt and pepper and toss to coat. In a large frying pan, heat butter and olive oil add beef and fry until brown on all sides. Add cognac, ingnite and stir until flam dies down. Place meat in a large casserole. In same frying pan, sauté pork lardons until they render their fat, remove and reserve. Add to skillet the next four ingredients and sauté until lightly browned, add the parsley and transfer to the casserole. In the frying pan add the red wine to deglaze the pan and pick up any brown bits, add this to the casserole this should cover the beef. If needed, add beef broth to just barely cover the beef. Bake in the oven at 350 for 1.5 hours then reduce to 300 for 1.5 hours.

NOTE: This dish is not to be consumed the first day. It is always better the following day.
Prepare Garnish:
2 lbs. pearl onion, peeled with ends removed
Butter
1 cup red wine
1 lb. mushroom caps, cleaned with stems removed
Butter and Olive oil
¼ cup cognac
Juice of ½ a lemon
Fresh parsley chopped

Melt butter in a sauté pan, add the onion and a very light sprinkle of sugar. Saute until golden brown on each side, add the red wine, cover and simmer minutes. Remove from pan.

Again in pan heat butter and olive oil and sauté mushroom caps until lightly browned. Add the cognac, ignite and extinguish with lemon juice. Toss until pan is deglazed.

To serve, place garnish on top of casserole, sprinkle with parsley and present casserole.

NOTE — We found that placing the serving portions in individual oven proof dishes made this easier to serve. We spooned cold Bourguignon into the individual dish and microwaved until just warm (approximately two to three minutes depending on your microwave). Add onion and mushroom garnish cover with foil and place in a 300 degree oven for an hour. If guests are not ready to be served, turn off the oven and they will remain warm for quite some time.

Purée de Pommes de Terre

3 to 4 large baking potatoes, quartered
8 oz. carton sour cream or crème fraiche
½ stick butter
Salt and white pepper

Place potatoes in boiling water and boil until you can pierce with a knife. Drain and immediately and with a potato ricer, rice the potatoes back into the hot pot. Microwave the butter and crème fraiche until melted and hot, add three small pinches of salt and a pinch of white pepper, and pour over potatoes. Whisk potatoes with a wire whisk until smooth, but do not over process.

Petit Pois de Campagne

4 slices of bacon
½ stick butter
I small bunch green onion, chopped including some of the green parts
4 to 6 leaves of Boston Bibb lettuce sliced chiffonade
I small can of peas
I 32 oz. bag of frozen peas (if you can get fresh peas this is ideal)

In a frying pan, sauté the bacon until thoroughly cooked but not crisp. Add butter and continue to sauté. Add onion and only the juice from the can of peas. Bring to a simmer and add the chiffonade lettuce. Add this sauce to the heated or steamed peas.

NOTE — You can use a large oval serving dish and place potatoes around the edge and the peas in the middle and pass them. It makes a very nice presentation.

Crepes Noisette et Chocolat Flambé

As a child, my parents took us to restaurants, which we loved because it was the only time we really had dessert. My siblings and I begged my father if we could have a flambé dessert. Cherries Jubilee or Crepes Suzette, PAHleaseeeee we would chime in unison! I loved all the fan fare and fire, and how nonchalant the waiter was about the entire task. Now, I know the waiter was probably doing a "Victory Dance" when we could not see.
Crepes filled with pureed hazelnuts and chocolate

6 crepes
6 tsp Hazelnut Butter
8 oz. cream
2 TB cocoa powder
3 TB sugar
6 TB water
I TB butter
3 TB cognac
3 TB hazelnut liqueur
¼ cup toasted hazel nuts, chopped

Take each crepe and place on a hot sauté pan until warm and pliable. Add one generous teaspoon of hazelnut puree and fold into half and half again forming a triangle.

In a chafing dish or large sauté pan add water and sugar and cook until caramelized. Add cream and cocoa allow to reduce (30 to 45 seconds or until it thickens), add cognac and flambé.

Add hazelnut liqueur and then the folded stuffed crepes and baste with chocolate sauce. Serve on hot plates with fresh whipped crème and toasted hazelnut garnish.

QUICK TIP We have made our own crepes and we have used the frozen ones you find in the supermarket. We find the results are equal. You can make your own crepes and freeze them. They freeze really well. Separate crepes with wax paper before freezing. NOTE: You can make your own hazelnut butter in the Vita-Mix following the manufactures' instructions. The flavor and richness this adds surpasses any commercial variety of hazelnut puree. You can also find Hazelnut butter in many health and natural food markets.

ALTERNATIVE

Crepe Suzette

6 French crepes, folded in quarters
3 TB sugar
6 TB water
¾ cup orange juice
Juice of half a lemon
I oz. butter
4 TB Grand Marnier
I wooden spatula
matches or a lighter

Make the caramel by placing a frying pan on a high heat, add the water and sugar and mix thoroughly. After two minutes it will begin to caramelize, add the butter and combine well. Then, add the orange juice and lemon juice and reduce for about 30 seconds to allow it to thicken.

Heat the crepes by placing the folded crepes into the frying pan and heat for I minute. Using the wooden spatula, move them in the sauce to soak them completely. It's important that the crepes are very hot to help the liquor ignite. Flambé the crepes by pouring the Grand Marnier into the frying pan and ignite using a lighter or a long match.

Place the crepes onto individual plates and pour some sauce over each one.

The crepes can be served as they are or with some caramelized orange peel and a dollop of whipped cream or ice cream.

Voilà!

Photo by Miro Slav OtraVista Photography, España

Bar mixers and Punches for a Crowd

Simple Syrup

1 cup sugar
1 cup water

Place sugar and water in a pan and stir to dissolve, bring to a boil. Remove from heat and cool completely. You can store this in a clean bottle and keep refrigerated for several days

Homemade Margarita Mix

1½ cups water
1½ cups sugar
2 cups fresh lime juice

Follow cooking directions for the simple syrup, after cooling completely add the lime juice and stir. This can be made several days in advance and even kept frozen so you always some on hand.

Sweet-n-Sour Mix

1½ cups water
1½ cups sugar
1 cup fresh lime juice
1 cup fresh lemon juice

Follow cooking directions for the simple syrup, after cooling completely add the juices and stir. This can be made several days in advance and even kept frozen so you always some on hand.

Piña Colada Mix

½ cup crème of coconut
1 cup pineapple juice

Mix in a blender and chill for up to three days. When ready just add rum and ice and blend until thick and slushy.

Champagne Punch

11 oz. apricot brandy
3 oz. grenadine
4 oz. pineapple juice
4 oz. lemon juice
1 bottle chilled dry white wine
2 bottles chilled champagne

Mix all the ingredients together and place in a punch bowl with a block of ice. Garnish with slices of lemon.

Fish House Punch

12 fresh lemons juiced
6 cups cognac
4 cups club soda
4 cups peach brandy
1 bottle Jamaican amber rum, 750 ml (fifth)
2 cups strong tea
1 cup light brown sugar

Mix the lemon juice and the sugar until dissolved. Add cognac, brandy and rum. Chill for three hours. Pour over a large block of ice in a punch bowl. Stir well then add the soda and tea. Stir well again. Garnish with sliced lemon. This punch makes approximately 40 servings unless my friend Greg is there and then it only serves 6.

Pimm's Number 1 Punch

We went to a large Spanish celebration with a group from Ireland and Denmark and the host served this punch from England. Talk about an International affair! I watched her make this punch and winced at the combination being poured into the punch bowl. The end result was a really nice refreshing punch and it is really easy to make.
1 bottle Pimms Cup number 1, 750ml (fifth)
2 liters ginger ale or lemon lime soda
1 cucumber
1 orange
1 lemon

Pour Pimms in a punch bowl with a block of ice. Add ginger ale or lemon-lime soda. Slice cucumber in half long ways and slice into $\frac{1}{8}$ inch slices creating half moons. Slice orange and lemon in the same manner and add the cucumber and fruit to the punch bowl.

Lessons Learned

The secret to fantastic cooking is using fresh ingredients!

If you need crème fraiche or sour cream but do not have any you can add one tablespoon of vinegar to every cup of cream and allow to sit at room temperature for an hour.

Before grating cheese if you oil the grater it is easier to clean.

If you need beef gravy to appear a little darker you can add a small amount of instant coffee.

Thaw fish in milk to remove the "frozen" taste and bring out the fresh caught flavor.

Pie crust won't be tough if you use milk instead of water and always work dough minimally and well chilled. A teaspoon of vinegar makes the crust flakier.

Before measuring honey or syrup, grease the spoon with a little butter to prevent sticking.

Freeze a surplus of limes or lemons and when you defrost you will get twice as much juice.

When making a chocolate cake, grease the pan and dust with cocoa to keep it brown.

If you over salt a dish, add one teaspoon cider vinegar and one teaspoon of sugar to remedy the situation the best you can.

Before boiling potatoes, rice or pasta rub butter around the top inside to prevent it from boiling over.

Fill ice trays with hot water to make them freeze faster (really).

Charcoal impregnated with fuel often makes food have a chemical taste. Use newspaper, sticks and small pieces of wood to start your BBQ however, if you must use liquid fuel, add to charcoal 10 minutes before lighting to absorb and be sure to burn until coals are gray-white to remove chemical taste.

Do not let anyone throw cigarette butts into your BBQ.

Wash you hands frequently with soap and hot water! To be sure you have washed your hands adequately, sing this song while washing, *"Oh a sailor sails the seven seas, he does whatever he pleases, BUT he always remember to wash his hands, so he won't get no diseases".*

Photo by Miro Slav OtraVista Photography, España

Culinary Vacation Holiday

Try a culinary vacation in Andalucia Spain's historic white village of Torrox Pueblo.

For a few weeks each year Casa Cebadillas in the historic village of Torrox Pueblo, Spain opens its kitchen and guest quarters for personalized cooking classes to a small number of guests eager to share in the food, wine, and culture of one of Spain's most diverse and vibrant regions of Andalucia.

Guests cook with wild Mediterranean herbs gathered from the garden, venture down the streets into local household salons for fresh salad greens, fruits and vegetables from local markets, olives from the local groves, and prepare unique Mediterranean, Sephardic, and Moorish-Arabic dishes. Included is a field trip to a local cortijo to watch the preparation of a meal from a local family. The grand finale is when the students plan and prepare a meal for a group of six locals!

The one week English language program includes hands-on cooking sessions led by Christopher Carnrick, as well as guided visits to markets, vineyards, shops, and local restaurants. All cooking programs take place in a manner to allow you free time to explore.

Each day's program offers something different; the prepared menus shared while taking in views of the white village of Torrox and the sea. In the background you can hear the goats and the herders in the distance and the smell of fresh roasting local chilies.

You will be given an insider's guide to the regional production of local olives and oil, cheese and wine as well as and tastings. All instruction is in English.

Recipes are geared for preparation at home once you return to showcase your new skills! Guests are supplied with supplies needed for the week.

The class is limited to 4 guests per week. The week begins with a tour of the village and a welcome dinner on Sunday night and ends after "graduation" dinner on Friday.

Christopher and Arthur have lived in Torrox for several years and are the creators of Casa Cebadillas, the Unique Dining Experience in Torrox Pueblo www.casa-cebadillas.com. Together they are eager to share with you some of the culinary discoveries they have made in this wonderful part of Andalucía. They offer a 6 night Culinary Experience Holiday which offers a more in-depth adventure into Andalucian cuisine including a venture into the Alpujarras and the finale is the participants prepare a meal for six locals!

Oven Temperature Conversion Chart

Fahrenheit (degrees F)	Celsius (degrees C)	Gas Number	Oven Terms
225 degrees F	110 degrees C	1/4	Very Cool
250 degrees F	130 degrees C	1/2	Very Slow
275 degrees F	140 degrees C	1	Very Slow
300 degrees F	150 degrees C	2	Slow
325 degrees F	165 degrees C	3	Slow
350 degrees F	177 degrees C	4	Moderate
375 degrees F	190 degrees C	5	Moderate
400 degrees F	200 degrees C	6	Moderately Hot
425 degrees F	220 degrees C	7	Hot
450 degrees F	230 degrees C	8	Hot
475 degrees F	245 degrees C	9	Hot
500 degrees F	260 degrees C	10	Extremely Hot
550 degrees F	290 degrees C	10	Broiling

Volume Conversion Chart

1 US tablespoon	=	3 US teaspoons
1 US fluid ounce	≅	29.57353 milliliters (ml)
1 US cup	=	16 US tablespoons
1 US cup	=	8 US fluid ounces
1 US pint	=	2 US cups
1 US pint	=	16 US fluid ounces
1 liter (l)	≅	33.8140227 US fluid ounces
1 liter (l)	=	1000 milliliters (ml)
1 US quart	=	2 US pints
1 US gallon	=	4 US quarts
1 US gallon	=	3.78541178 liters

Weight Conversion

1 milligram (mg)	=	0.001 grams (g)
1 gram (g)	=	0.001 kilograms (kg)
1 gram (g)	≅	0.035273962 ounces
1 ounce	=	28.34952312 grams (g)
1 ounce	=	0.0625 pounds
1 pound (lb)	=	16 ounces
1 pound (lb)	=	0.45359237 kilograms (kg)
1 kilogram (kg)	=	1000 grams
1 kilogram (kg)	≅	35.273962 ounces
1 kilogram (kg)	≅	2.20462262 pounds (lb)
1 stone	=	14 pounds

Conversion Factors

Ounces to grams: Multiply ounce figure by 28.3 to get grams

Pounds to grams: Multiply pound figure by 453.59 to get grams

Pounds to kilograms: Multiple pound figure by 0.45 to get kilograms

Ounces to milliliters: Multiple ounce figure by 30 to get milliliters

Cups to liters: Multiple cup figure by 0.24 to get number of liters

Fahrenheit to Celsius: Subtract 32 from F number multiply by 5, then divide by 9, to get Celsius number. You can also use our on-line SUPER CONVERTER by visiting www.spain-vacation-holiday.com

Have a question on a particular theme? Write us and we will give you the best answer we can!

casa-cebadillas@spain-vacation-holiday.com

Made in the USA
Charleston, SC
13 April 2012